LATIN FOR READING

A Beginner's Textbook with Exercises

REVISED EDITION

Glenn M. Knudsvig, Gerda M. Seligson, and Ruth S. Craig

Instructor's Manual

Preliminary Edition, Fall 1986

Ann Arbor   The University of Michigan Press

Introduction

If you already teach Latin or are about to teach it for the first time, you are most likely a person who loves the classics and you have a talent for language. Chances are the majority of the students who will enroll in your class will not match this description. They or their parents have heard that Latin is good for one. They also have heard that it is hard and that they will probably forget it the instant they stop studying it, but that like chin-ups, jogging or spinach it is really good for one. And so it is. Even if they forget the details of Latin grammar sooner or later, they will remember their experience with a language system that is so significantly different from their own.

The main motivation for the linguistic research conducted at The University of Michigan (research which, begun in 1953, has produced five published and several unpublished textbooks for elementary Latin) has always been a concern for the continued decline in the quality of student translation from Latin. This decline was characteristic of the second quarter of this century and seems to have continued in many schools. The replacement on national tests of passages for translation by passages for analysis and comprehension was a shocking manifestation of this decline. Translation seemed to become increasingly difficult, if not impossible, for many students.

This surely had not been the intention of the members of the famous Classical Investigation who, in the twenties, officially changed the goal of teaching Latin from writing to reading, but it was its unforeseen result. For, although the leaders of the profession changed the goal, they did not--with a few notable exceptions--give any positive advice on how to renew and adapt old procedures to meet the new goals. The descriptions of Latin and the rules to be learned remained the same as they had been: descriptions and rules for writing correct Latin.

The tradition from which almost all Latin (and Greek) textbooks derive is very old. Its goal was to equip the student with the tools to understand, speak and write Latin as a medium of communication. It did so, often very successfully. It stressed that:

1. the parts of the sentence must be in a certain form.
2. the logical relationships between clauses must be expressed by certain conjunctions and moods.
3. the main subject matter must be the study of morphology, syntax, and logical relations.
4. the study of vocabulary is a necessary condition for understanding, speaking and writing.

Since direct understanding, speaking and writing have been abandoned, reading, which in some settings had been an almost involuntary by-product, has become the main objective of teaching Latin. Needless to say, it is still necessary to study vocabulary, morphology, syntax and logical relations, but their study is not sufficient for reading. The pragmatic situation of the reader is different from that of the speaker/writer. Speakers/writers start out with a thought, idea, sentiment: they know what they want to say. Readers do not know what the specific message is that they will receive. That is the significant difference. To deal with this situation, readers must be given some strategies that were not required for the attainment of the traditional goals. We have made it our business to analyze the situation of the readers. The result is a strategy established in the first five chapters of our textbook. The remaining lessons apply and reapply the principles and assumptions in the manner of a learning spiral.

The situation of readers is characterized by expectancy. To begin with, readers expect a speech act or acts to take place. Their situation is similar to that of a person receiving a phone call. The caller is expected to ask a question, make a request, pass on a piece of information, etc. He or she is expected to perform a speechact. If no speechact is forthcoming, the person who has been called becomes justifiably irritated because his or her normal expectation has not been fulfilled. Next, the speechact is expected to be understandable, i.e., complete. A native speaker knows instinctively when a speechact is complete (although possibly abbreviated), and when it is not. The would-be reader of a foreign language has no such instinctive knowledge. Learning to read a foreign language means to acquire the skills necessary to produce a facsimile of the native speaker's instinctive knowledge.

Overview of Lessons One through Five

The unit of written language that most closely resembles a speechact is the independent clause or sentence. Its minimum form is the kernel, introduced in lesson one and kept up for use as an anchor for all reading. The kernel, not the word or phrase, is the unit that must be expected by the reader. There are several types of kernels in Latin. Our analysis makes use of seven types. A different analysis might operate with a smaller or larger number. A famous European grammarian lists more than 300. Lessons one through five introduce two kernel types only, names according to the type of the verb: transitive active and intransitive active. The concept of verb typology is crucial for forming correct expectations about the completeness of a kernel and must be kept up as well as the kernal concept. The by-now commonly accepted practice of listing the fourth principal part of a verb as ending in -us, -a-, -um when transitive, but in -um or -urus when intransitive is helpful. Speechacts are pragmatic events, not syntactical constructions. There are no transitive or intransitive speechacts, only transitive or intransitive kernels. Speechacts, called modes of speech in lesson three, can be recognised easily in the first five lessons by their punctuation marks, so far periods and question-marks. Learners must be trained to watch carefully for information at the kernel level.

In contrast to the kernel, which must be expected, connection need never be expected. Nevertheless, it is crucial to respect and be aware of coordinating connection. It means that an expectation that has already been fulfilled is to be fulfilled once more and that what follows has to be considered a repetition that is syntactically dispensable. A surprising number of mistakes in translation are the consequence of mishandling or ignoring connection.

Gapping, also introduced in lesson two, likewise needs never to occur. It is a stylistic device, a kind of shorthand with different languages using different systems of shorthand, and different speakers making more or less use of their shorthand system. Just as lack of respect for the coordinating conjunction can be fatal for reading, so is lack of respect for the gap. In traditional Latin literature gaps are very frequent. That is the reason why in this textbook gapping is introduced in the second lesson, and why a gapping problem should appear on almost every test.

To read modification structures successfully it is necessary to expect a verb as head of an adverbial modifier (lesson four with other heads later) and nouns and pronouns as heads of adjectival modifiers (lesson five). The concept of semantic features and categories that is introduced in lesson four is well-known and used in traditional textbooks. However it has rarely been utilized for reading purposes. It is very helpful for making educated guesses.

The last concept necessary for reading is only hinted at in these lessons, but it is important for all reading. This is the concept of syntactical equivalents. If students understand that a noun clause fulfills the same expectation as a noun, a pronoun or a verbal noun and that an adjectival clause fulfills the same expectation as an adjective, a genitive, etc., the number of the expectations students have to hold becomes rather small. They can then easily use them as the helps in reading that they really are.

These then, to sum up, are the concepts and expectations established in the first five lessons:

    speechacts (statements and questions)
    the kernel
    connection
    the gap
    modification
    semantic features
    syntactic equivalents

They apply equally to Latin and English and a native speaker uses them instinctively, all the time, but a foreigner must operate them consciously. Unless students are made and kept aware of them, these concepts and the notion of expectations cannot become useful in learning to read Latin. This textbook is constructed for this very purpose. These seven concepts and expectations comprise the 'something else' that usually was not taught in traditional textbooks because it was not necessary for the purposes of the speaker/writer. For the reader this 'something else' is indispensable.

Contents

Table 1. Case Use by Lesson Number

Lesson	Nominative	Accusative	Ablative	Dative	Genitive
1	Subject	Direct Object			
4			W/Prep.: Manner Place Frequency Accompaniment		
5	Neuter	Neuter	Neuter		
6			Means Agent		
10	Subject complement	Object complement			
12		Adverbial			
15			Absolute		
16				Special Intransitive Special Linking Reference Purpose W/est Indirect Object Compound Verbs W/Adjectives	
17					Possessive Subjective Objective Partitive Descriptive
22		Ad+Gerund			Causa+Gerund
23		Object Infinitive Indirect Statement			
25			Comparison		
35				Agent	

Table 2. Modification by Lesson Number

Lesson	Adjectival	Adverbial
4		Adverbs Preposition with the Ablative
5	Adjective	
6		Ablative w/o preposition
11		Dependent clauses in indicative: cum, dum, postquam, quia, si, ubi, ut
12		Accusatives w/prepositions Accusatives w/o prepositions
13	Relative Clauses	
14	Participial Clauses	
15		Ablative Absolute
17	Noun in the Genitive	
20	Special Adjectives	
33	Relative Clause of Purpose Relative Clause of Characteristic	Result Clauses Purpose Clauses
34		Clause of circumstance Clause of concession Clause of proviso

Table 3. Subordinate Clauses by Lesson Number

Lesson	Noun	Adjectival	Adverbial

11			Causal: quod
			          quia
			Condition: si
			          (+ indic.)
			Temporal: Postquam
			          Ut
			          Ubi
			          Dum
			Comparison:
			          Ut
			Place: Ubi

13	Relative:
	  quicumque, etc.
		Relative: qui
		          quae
		          quod
		            etc.	

14		Participial	
15			Ablative Absolute
23	Objective Infinitive Indirect Statement		
30	Indirect Question		
31	Indirect Comm.		
32	Noun Result Clause of Fearing		

33		Relative Clause of
		  Characteristic
		Relative Clause of
		  Purpose
			Clause of Result
			Clause of Purpose

34			Circumstance: cum Time: cum, dum Cause: cum Concession: cum Proviso: dum Condition: Simple: Potential Contrary-to-fact

Table 4. Nouns by Lesson Number

Lesson	I	II	III	IV	V
1.	hōra īra	animus	fūr occāsiō vēritās	manus successus	rēs spēs
2.	avāritia fēmina fortūna pecūnia sapientia vīta	lupus populus vir	homō nox	senātus	diēs
4.	cūra harēna	amīcus cōnsilium locus modus stultus	gladiātor prūdēns		
5.	aqua	perīculum vīnum vitium	amor corpus culmen fīnis fōns imitātiō mēns opus		
6.	causa	aper auxilium	canis multitūdō ratiō tempus	impetus	
7.	lacrima	āctum deus	fēlīcitās		
8.		astrum	animal mare mōs mūnus piscis vulpēs		
9.	ālea cōpia nātūra	ager castra	ars Caesar		aciēs
10.		oculus	dux necessitūdō		
11.	mora	Crassus	Carbō condiciō		glaciēs
12.	jānua Rōma	annus verbum	cor urbs	domus	

	I	II	III	IV	V
13.		exemplum Rōmulus	līs māter nōmen pater		
14.	littera stēlla	somnus	fax lūx vōx		
15.		Bellovacī	flūmen obses	exercitus	
16.	Mūsa poēta	beneficium impedīmentum	cīvitās honor salūs sōlitūdō	ūsus	
17.	domina jūstitia rēgīna	virtūs	imāgō index	vultus	
18.			necessitās ōs		
19.	puella	studium	laus		
20.			lībertās nēmō		
21.	amīcitia		lītus		
22.			hostis timor	sēnsus	
23.			mīles pōns		
24.			victor		
25.	Belgae	Gallus speculum	aedes leō plūs		
26.	lūna via	caelum	custōs sīdus		
27.			āctiō voluntās		
28.			ops		
29.			ōrātiō		
30.		fātum			

	I	II	III	IV	V
31.		Helvētiī	līmes Orgetorīx		
32.		bellum fīnitimī	uxor	metus	
33.			probitās vīs		
34.		tribūnus	ōrdō		
35.	silva		pēs tellūs voluptās		

Table 5. Verbs by Lesson Number

	I	II	III	III -io	IV	Irr.
1.	lavō		alō vincō	faciō fugiō	impediō	
2.	irrītō satiō		cognōscō premō regō			
3.	amō	audeō dēbeō soleō videō	agō	cupiō	audiō	possum volō
4.	ambulō		vīvō	capiō	pereō veniō	sum
5.	adjuvō corōnō intrō	habeō	dēfluō vānēscō			
6.		teneō	āmittō dūcō mittō			offerō
7.	cūrō		fallō frangō neglegō pāscō			
8.						
9.	aedificiō dō	doceō	īnstruō prōdūcō	jaciō		
10.	appellō vocō					fīō
11.			discō			intereō
12.		doleō pateō	cōgō fundō			
13.			condō resolvō			
14.		maneō	currō invādō scrībō		sepeliō	
15.			crēscō fluō	accipiō		
16.	mōnstrō nārrō	faveō noceō placeō	crēdō dīcō impōnŏ		serviō	adsum dēsum

7

	I	II	III	III -io	IV	Irr.
16.			inicere parcō resistō			
17.						
18.	errō jūdicō laudō		quaerō	effugiō		eō ferō mālō nōlō
19.	accūsō		trahō			
20.	imitor mīror	gaudeō timeō vereor	cadō dīco īrāscor loquor morior nāscor patior sequor ūtor		mentior	
21.	juvō labōrō ōrō	decet licet moneō oportet	concēdō dēpōnō dēserō relinquō			
22.	cōgitō				nesciō	
23.	arbitror nārrō negō putō vetō	jubeō prohibeō			sciō sentiō	
24.	superō					
25.			emō reddō			
26.	līberō	fulgeō			custōdiō inveniō	
27.						
28.			contendō			
29.	postulō spērō			rapiō		
30.	interrogō rogō		requīrō			

	I	II	III	III -io	IV	Irr.
31.	hortor imperō precor	cēnseō persuādeō suādeō	cōnstituō permittō sinō statuō			exeō
32.			accidō metuō	efficiō		īnferō
33.			dēligō edō			
34.	mātūrō nūntiō	valeō	concidō proficīscor			ōdī
35.	pūgnō pulsō repudiō	egeō	bibō cernō spernō			adeō

Table 6. Adjectives by Lesson Number

Lesson	I and II	III
5.	amīcus bonus magnus malus novus parvus pulcher pūrus quantus stultus	absēns facilis fortis omnis quālis
7.	hūmānus multus	crūdēlis fēlix
8.		levis
9.	dīvīnus	
10.	longus timidus	brevis sapiēns
11.	crassus	fragilis
12.	singulī tantus	
13.	suus	inops
16.	aptus cārus grātus honestus inimīcus nūllus proximus	Athēniēnsēs dissimilis Plataeēnsēs similis
18.	caecus meus noster tuus vester	
19.	alius	
20.	alter līber neuter sōlus tōtus ūllus uter uterque	

10

	I and II	III
21.	Dōricus proprius vērus	difficilis
25.	maximus minimus mortuus optimus pessimus plūrimus vīvus	dīves gracilis humilis intolerābilis nōbilis plūrēs tālis
26.	serenus	
27.	rēctus	
28.	avārus lepidus verbōsus	
30.	Christiānus	
31.	medius	
34.	prīmus reliquus	ācer mīlitāris
35.	antīquus prīvātus	

Table 7. Indeclinables by Lesson Number

Less.	Prepositions	Adverbs	Subordinating & Coordinating Conjunctions*	Question Words & Other**
2.		nōn	et (c) sed (c) -que (c)	
3.				-ne
4.	ā/ab (abl.) cum (abl.) dē (abl.) ē/ex (abl.) in (abl.) sine (abl.)	fēliciter fidēliter fortiter numquam semper rectē		quō ā/dē/ē locō quō (in) locō quōcum quō modō quotiēns ubi unde
6.	ā/ab (abl.)	aegrē facile saepe		ā quō quā dē causā quandō quō auxiliō quō tempore
8.				centum (number) decem " mīlle " octō " quattor " quīnque " septem " sex " novem " quot
9.	prō (abl.)			
10.				etiam (intensifier)
11.			cum (s) dum (s) postquam (s) quia (s) quod (s) sī (s) ut (s) ubi (s)	cūr quā condiciōne

less.	Prepositions	Adverbs	Conjunctions	Question Words and Other
12.	sub (abl., acc.) ad (acc.) ante (acc.) contrā (acc.) in (acc.) inter (acc.) intrā (acc.) ob (acc.) per (acc.) post (acc.) praeter (acc.) prope (acc.) propter (acc.) sub (acc.) super (acc.) suprā (acc.) trans (acc.)	ante contrā intus multum nihil plūs post super suprā tantum	atque (c)	quam diū quantum quem ad locum quō quō factō nihil (indecl. noun)
13.		cito		nil (indecl. noun)
16.		bis celeriter		et (intensifier)
21.		subitō	et...et (c)	
25.		ibi ita tam totiēns	quam (c)	tot (indecl. adj.)
26.			aut (c) aut...aut (c)	
29.		certē fortisan utinam nē		
30.				an nōnne num utrum..an
31.			nē (s)	
33.		adeō		
34.		hīc quoque tamen	antequam (s) dōnec (s) dummodo (s) etsī (s) ni (s) priusquam (s)	autem (sentence conn.) igitur (sentence conn.)

Less.	Prepositions	Adverbs	Conjunctions	Question Words and Other
34 (con't.)			quamquam (s)	
			quamvīs (s)	
			quasi (s)	
			quoad (s)	
			quoniam (s)	
			simul at (s)	
			sīn (s)	
			sīve (s)	
			sīve...sīve (c)	
35.		ācriter	vel (c)	
		nunc		
		praeterea		
		precāriō		
		vel		

* (c) = coordinating conjunction
  (s) = subordinating conjunction

** all words in this column are question words unless otherwise noted

14

List of All Indeclinables from Lesson Vocabulary and Readings

Prepositions + ablative

a/ab	from	(4)
cum	with	(4)
de	from, down from; concerning	(4)
e/ex	from, out of	(4)
in	in, on	(4)
sine	without	(4)
a/ab	by	(6)
pro	before, in front of; for, on behalf of.	(9)
sub	under	(12)

Prepositions + accusative

ad	to, toward	(12)
ante	in front of; before	(12)
contra	against	(12)
extra	outside of	(12)
in	into, onto	(12)
inter	between, among	(12)
intra	within	(12)
ob	against; because of	(12)
per	through	(12)
post	behind, after	(12)
praeter	in addition to; except	(12)
prope	near	(12)
propter	because of	(12)
sub	under	(12)
super	over, above	(12)
supra	above, over	(12)
trans	across	(12)
*apud	in the presence of; among	(31)

Adverbs

non (2)
fideliter (4)
fortiter (4)
numquam (4)
semper (4)
aegre (4)
facile (6)
saepe (6)
jam (7)
*tandem (8)
deinde (RL2)
ante (12)
contra (12)
diu (12)
intus (12)

multum (12)
nihil (12)
post (12)
super (12)
supra (12)
tantum (12)
cito (13)
*mox (13)
maxime (RL3)
subito (RL3)
quoque (RL3)
*primum (14)
*statim (14)
*tum (14)
bis (16)
celeriter (16)
subito (21)
*satis (22)
*sic (22)
ibi (25)
ita (25)
tam (25)
totiens (25)
*olim (26)
*nunc (27)
certe (29)
fortisan (29)
utinam (29)
*bene (31)
adeo (33)
hic (34)
quoque (34)
tamen (34)
nunc (35)
praeterea (35)
precario (35)
vel (35)

Number Words

centum (8)
decem (8)
mille (8)
octo (8)
quattuor (8)
quinque (8)
septem (8)
sex (8)
novem (8)

Coordinating Conjunctions

et (2)
sed (2)
-que (2)

atque (12)
*nec (24)
quam (25)
nec (26)
*at (27)
*neque (29)
vel (35)

Subordinating Conjunctions

cum (11)
dum (11)
postquam (11)
quia (11)
quod (11)
si (11)
ut (11)
nisi (27)
ne (29)
antequam (34)
donec (34)
dummondo (34)
etsi (34)
ni (34)
priusquam (34)
quamquam (34)
quamvis (34)
quasi (34)
quoad (34)
quoniam (34)
simul ac (34)
sin (34)
sive (34)

Sentence Connectors

*autem (8)
itaque (RL2)
ergo (29)
nam (29)
autem (34)
igitur (34)

Qestion Words

-ne (3)
quo a/de/e loco (4)
quo (in) loco (4)
quocum (4)
quo modo (4)
quotiens (4)
ubi (4)
unde (4)
a quo (6)
qua de causa (6)

quando (6)
quo auxilio (6)
quo tempore (6)
quot (8)
cur (11)
ubi (11)
qua condicione (11)
quam diu (12)
quantum (12)
quem ad locum (12)
quo (12)
quo facto (12)
an (30)
nonne (30)
ne (30)

Intensifiers

etiam (10)
*quidem (10)

Indeclinable Nouns

nihil (12)
nil (13)
satis (22)

Indeclinable Adjectives

satis (22)
tot (25)

* = Words occuring in readings only, not in lesson vocabulary.

16

Lesson 1

Establish the following:

-parts of speech: noun and verb
-subject and direct object
-morphology, morpheme
-morphology of Latin noun and verb
-Latin noun paradigm
        -nominative case
        -accusative case
-form identification
-the complete sentence
-the kernel
-technique of metaphrasing
-expectations

Readings

1.   Brevity pleases.
2.   Time reveals the truth.
3.   Time diminishes grief.
4.   One lawsuit creates another.
5.   A beard does not make a philosopher.
6.   Affection creates affection.
7.   Necessity has (knows) no law.

Supplementary Exercise, Lesson 1

Directions: Given the following dictionary entries, identify each of the
    items below. Be sure to list part of speech and include all
    possibilities.

I.   succēdo, succēdere: to go under: to approach; to submit
          successus, successūs: success

1. succēdit
2. successum
3. successus
4. successum

II.   vincō, vincere: to conquer
          victor, victōris: conqueror, victor

1. vincit
2. victor
3. victōrem

III.   alō, alere: to feed, nourish
          āla, ālae: wing

1. alit
2. ālam
3. āla

SO FAR	BEGINNING WITH THIS LESSON
(Content covered in previous lessons that will serve as a starting point for content introduced in the current lesson--see next column.)	
-parts of speech: noun and verb	-part of speech: coordinating conjunction
-one of the big 3 categories used in describing the components of a sentence, the kernel.	-another of the big 3: connectors (The third of the big 3, modifiers, will first appear in lesson 4.)
-Words in a sentence are parts of the kernel.	-Words in a sentence are part of the kernel or are connectors.
-Each complete sentence has at least one clause and therefore at least one kernel.	-A sentence may have more than one clause and therefore more than one kernel.
-idea of completeness of expression	-The gap: words necessary for completeness are not always expressed.
-expectations based on the idea of completeness	-expectations of gapped items
-Any item of the kernel raises the expectation of other parts.	-An item expected may have been gapped but can be recovered from another clause.

ALL NEW

-connection

MAINTAIN

-(topics, concepts, facts other than those mentioned above must be maintained throughout the lesson)
-nominative, accusative morphology
-form identification

Readings

1. A friend seeks material aid, not the expectation of it.
2. A man adorns his position, the position does not adorn the man.
3. The physician gives care, nature heals.
4. Now brother deceives brother, now daughter (deceives) mother, (and now father), (deceives) son, (and) now friend (deceives) friend.
5. The fox wants deceit (trickery), the wolf (wants) a lamb, the woman (wants) praise.
6. The wolf changes his skin, but not his mind.

Supplementary Exercise, Lesson 2

Directions: Given the following dictionary entries, identify each of the items below. Be sure to list part of speech and include all possibilities.

I.   rēx, rēgis: king
       regō, regere: to rule, guide, direct
       regnō, regnāre: to have royal power; to be supreme

1. rēgem
2. regit
3. regnat
4. rēx

II.   irrītō, irrītāre: to provoke, enrage
       irrītātiō, irrītātiōnis: incitement, irritation, stimulant
       irrītātor, irritatōris: an inciter, instigator

1. irrītat
2. irrītātiōnem
3. irrītātor
4. irrītātiō
5. irrītātōrem

SO FAR	BEGINNING WITH THIS LESSON
-parts of speech	-a subclass (infinitive) of a part of speech (verb) or--if you prefer--a new part of speech (infinitive)
-infinitive as a dictionary item	-first use of infinitive
-morphology of finite verb	-morphology of the infinitive, a non-finite verb
-verb of kernel as single finite form	-Verb of kernel may be combination of a finite and a non-finite verb.
-lists of Latin vocabulary by part of speech	-the first of many specialized sub-lists of vocabulary (here, verbs that pattern with complementary infinitives) grouped according to morphological and/or semantic and/or syntactic criteria
-statements	-questions

ALL NEW

-semantic features: animate and non-animate nouns

MAINTAIN:

-idea of completeness
-complete kernel
-expectations
      (e.g., an infinitive raises the
      expectation of certain verbs at
      this stage and vice versa.)
-metaphrasing
-morphology of each part of speech
-form identification
-connection
-gapping

Directions: Given the following dictionary entries, identify each of the
    items below. Be sure to list part of speech and include all
    possibilities.

I.   agō, agere: to do, act, drive, lead
            alō, alere: to feed, nourish
            āla, ālae: wing

1. agit
2. alit
3. ālam
4. agere
5. alere

II.   cupiō, cupere: to desire, wish
            cupīdō, cupīdinis: desire, wish, longing
            cupītor, cupītōris: one who desires, wishes

1. cupere
2. cupitōrem
3. cupit
4. cupīdenem
5. cupīdō

SO FAR	BEGINNING WITH THIS LESSON
-parts of speech: noun, verb, conjunction, pronoun (interrogative)	-parts of speech: adverb and preposition
-two of the big 3 categories used in describing components of a sentence: kernel items and connectors	-the third of the big 3: modifiers (From now on each word in the sentence can be classified as a kernel item, connector, and/or modifier.)
-two cases of the Latin noun: nominative and accusative (three if you have introduced genitive)	-another case of the Latin noun: the ablative
-semantic feature of words	-additional semantic feature and categories of vocabulary items
-expectations within kernel	-A modifier raises expectations of a head.
-metaphrasing guidelines	-additional metaphrasing guidelines

ALL NEW

-modification

MAINTAIN (among other things)

-the sentence
-kernel
-idea of completeness
-connectors vs. kernel items
-expectations
-metaphrasing
-gapping

Readings

1.   A snake is hiding in the grass.
2.   No one lives without wrongdoing.
3.   No one always lives right.
4.   Troy falls from its height.
5.   A fool can live happily with a fool.
6.   The palm (of victory) does not come without dust.
7.   Gently in manner, forcefully in reality.

Supplementary Exercise, Lesson 4

Directions: Given the following dictionary entries, identify each of the
items below. Be sure to list part of speech and include all
possibilities.

I.   cūra, cūrae: care, concern
            currus, currūs: a chariot, car
            cūrō, cūrāre: to care for, cure

1. cūrā
2. cūrat
3. currū
4. currum
5. cūram
6. cūrō

II.   locus, locī: place, position
            locō, locāre: to place, arrange
            locātiō, locātiōnis: an arrangement

1. locum
2. locat
3. locātiō
4. locō
5. locātiōnem
6. locāre

<u>SO FAR</u>   <u>BEGINNING</u> <u>WITH</u> <u>THIS</u> <u>LESSON</u>

-Words in a sentence are items   -Some words are adjectival modifiers.
within kernels, are connectors,
or are adverbial modifiers.

-parts of speech   -add adjectives

-Nouns are identified by case and   -Add gender to identification.
number.

-Expectations: a modifier raises   -An adjective raises expectations of
the expectation of a head.   a noun-head.

-Gapping: identical items may   -applies to noun heads of adjectives
be gapped.   also (see S. 5.4)

ALL NEW

-agreement (by case, number, gender)

MAINTAIN

-the sentence
-metaphrasing and expectations
-Latin as a language which one can learn to read

Required readings

1.   Time flies.
2.   Smooth speech has its own poison.
3.   A sound mind in a sound body.
4.   Good wine gladdens the human heart.
5.   Common danger creates harmony (concord).
6.   Good clothes ennoble a stupid man.

Optional readings

7.   In wine, in anger, (or) in a child there is always truth.
8.   Troy falls from its great (lofty) height.
9.   Prosperity doesn't always have an accessible ear.
10.   Deception often lurks under a fair appearance.
11.   Deceit reigns in the lofty palace.
12.   A wise man does not live properly (honorably) in beautiful clothes.

Supplementary Exercise, Lesson 5

Directions: Given the following dictionary entries, identify each of the
     items below. Be sure to list part of speech and include all
     possibilities.

I.   coronō, coronāre, coronāvī, coronātus: to crown
            corona, coronae, f.: a garland or wreath; a crown

1. coronat
2. coronam
3. coronāre
4. coronā
5. corona

II.   sapiēns (sapientis): wise
            sapientia, sapientiae, f.: wisdom

1. sapientiam
2. sapiēns
3. sapientem
4. sapientiā
5. sapientī

33

Narrative reading

A wicked wolf wants a lamb, but a good shepherd is guarding the flock with great care. The wolf however makes a plan and puts upon himself a sheep's skin. The shepherd does not recognize the disguise and the wolf spends the night with the woolly flock. Now the hungry shepherd wants to get a lamb. He quickly seizes from the sheepfold a lamb--but the shepherd not knowing holds in his hand the wolf, not a lamb. And so the shepherd kills the wolf instead of a lamb.

The trick deceives the shepherd, but kills the wolf.

SO FAR	BEGINNING WITH THIS LESSON
-Clauses have one of two kernel types.	a third kernel type
-Adverbial modifiers are of two types.	a third type of adverbial modifier
-one of the uses of ablative case: object of preposition	-nouns in ablative case without a preposition
-Semantic categories/features influence interpretation of words/phrases	-new semantic categories/features and new interpretations based on this information [new metaphrase guidelines]

ALL NEW

-voice as a working term

MAINTAIN

-modifiers raise expectation of heads.
-the sentence, etc.

1.   Nothing is taught or learned properly (correctly) without (an)
      example.
2.   The poor man is honorably clad in old clothes.
3.   Through wine beauty perishes, through wine youth is corrupted.
4.   A sure friend is discovered in an unsure situation.
5.   Fire is nourished by wind, but it is (also) extinguished by wind.

Optional readings

6.   A jug is never carried honestly under (one's) coat.
7.   Power is bought by courage alone.
8.   Evil is often sought after, good is often shunned.
9.   Wisdom is overshadowed by wine.

Narrative reading

        A hungry and thirsty fox is wandering in a garden. Suddenly she
catches sight of a sweet bunch of grapes on a high vine, and she wants very
much to have it. She jumps with great hope, but can not/is not able to touch
it. Then she runs and jumps higher but she can not get the grapes. Finally
she goes away arrogantly and says: "Who wants to eat sour grapes? Not I."

        Man often despises that which he can not get.

Supplementary Exercise, Lesson 6

Directions: Given the following dictionary entries, identify each of the
      items below. Be sure to list part of speech and include all
      possibilities.

I.   canis, canis, m.: dog
            canō, canere: to sing
            canōrus, canōra, canōrum: melodious, harmonious

1. canitur
2. canōrum
3. canō
4. canōrō
5. cane
6. canī
7. canem

II.   teneō, tenēre: to hold; to keep
            tenuis, tenue: fine, thin; trifling

1. tenuem
2. tenuī
3. tenēre
4. tenētur
5. tenet
6. tenērī

SO FAR	BEGINNING WITH THIS LESSON
-nouns, adjectives, verbs in singular number (--i.e., show singular morphology)	-can be plural (i.e., show plural morphology)

-agreement

agreement in number
-subject-verb
-noun-adjective

-parts of speech

-a new pronoun

MAINTAIN

-the sentence
-Kernel information is unchanged.
-Modifiers are unchanged.
-Connectors are unchanged.
-expectations

Required readings

1.   At a prosperous time, many friends are counted.
2.   One's personality lives in one's eyes.
3.   Hard work nourishes noble minds.
4.   Truth and courage conquer.
5.   Religion cultivates gods, superstition violates them.
6.   Prosperity has many friends.

Optional readings

7.   Each beast crowns its own children with praise.
8.   The shipwrecked man is afraid even of quiet waters.
9.   Many diseases are cured by abstinence.
10.   Literature does not give/earn bread.
11.   Wealth brings cares.
12.   The eyes begin a love affair, familiarity completes it.

Narrative reading

A tortoise, because he is laughed at by other animals, challenges a hare to a contest. The hare laughs arrogantly, and says: "The race is already finished!" The other animals, however, set up the race and make the fox the judge. The fox gives the (starting) signal with a barking. The hare and the tortoise go forth from the starting place. The hare skims over the top of the sand on swift foot, but the tortoise proceeds on slow foot.

The hare leaves the tortoise far behind him (his back). Soon he stops (checks his step) and waits for the tortoise. Finally he lies down sleepy and goes to sleep.

Meanwhile the tortoise is proceeding with a slow and steady step. He passes the sleeping hare and approaches the goal. Suddenly the hare is aroused from sleep, but can no longer win (the race). Sadly he departs from the field. The fox and other animals proclaim and praise the victor.

Speed and arrogance are conquered/overcome by perseverance.

Supplementary Exercise, Lesson 7

Directions: Given the following dictionary entries, identify each of the
    items below. Be sure to list part of speech and include all
    possibilities.

I.   cūra, cūrae, f.: care, concern
            cūrō, cūrāre: to care for
            curtus, curta, curtum: shortened, broken, mutilated

1. cūrat
2. cūrantur
3. cūrārī
4. cūrīs
5. curta
6. curtum
7. cūrō
8. cūram

II.   fallācia, fallāciae, f.: deceit, trick
            fallax (fallācis): deceitful
            fallō, fallere: to deceive, harm

1. fallāciā
2. fallācī
3. fallitur
4. fallunt
5. fallācem
6. fallāciae
7. fallī

SO FAR

-plural morphology of first and
second declension nouns and
adjectives

BEGINNING WITH THIS LESSON

-plural morphology of third, fourth and
fifth declension nouns and adjectives

_____

ALL NEW

-cardinal numbers

MAINTAIN

-See lesson 7

Required readings

1.   Stupid persons fear fortune, wise ones bear it.
2.   Fortune helps the brave.
3.   Jupiter rules all things/everything in the sky, Caesar rules all
       things/everything on earth.
4.   The gods look at mortal acts with just eyes.
5.   The Roman state stands because of its ancient customs and men.
6.   Evil associations corrupt good manners.
7.   Fish are caught in the big ocean.

Optional readings

8.   Time reveals all things.
9.   Human beings drink wine, all other animals drink water.
10.   Fire tests gold, misfortune tests brave men.
11.   One night (death) waits for us all/all persons.
12.   The hours indeed pass and the days and the months and the years, and
       past time never returns.
13.   What do unenforced laws accomplish without (the moral) customs (of
       society)?

Narrative reading

        An old man and his son are walking on the road with a little donkey.
Soon two girls see them. One girl says, "Look! The stupid men have a donkey,
but they are proceeding on foot and are not being carried by the animal.
Three donkeys, not one, are walking!" Then the son climbs upon the donkey,
and they proceed, the son on the donkey, the father on foot.

Then three old men see them. One speaks for all (three), "O the times, O the manners! Where is (our) ancient <u>pietas</u>?" The son is affected with great grief (is very sorry), and he dismounts and proceeds on foot. His father climbs up on the donkey.

Then two women with one voice accuse the father, because his little son endures such great (hard) labor. Therefore the old man places his son also upon the donkey. Both father and son are sitting on the donkey.

Soon, however, a traveler murmurs, "The donkey is so small. Why are men being carried by a donkey? Why are strong men not walking? Why don't they carry the animal?" Both father and son are affected by his words. Both dismount and the two men carry the little animal. Everyone laughs because the men are so stupid.

Finally the father says, "Nothing is approved by all (the people)." Therefore they put down the donkey, and they all proceed on foot with great joy.

Supplementary Exercise, Lesson 8

Directions: Given the following dictionary entries, identify each of the items below. Be sure to list part of speech and include all possibilities.

I.   animal, animālis, n.: animal
        animus, animī, m.: mind
        anima, animae, f.: wind; breath; the breath of life, soul

1. animīs
2. animālia
3. anima
4. animālī
5. animōs
6. animam

II.   levamentum, levamentī, m.: alleviation, consolation
        levis, leve: light, unstable, fickle
        levō, levāre: to relieve, console

1. levibus
2. levēs
3. levātur
4. levamenta
5. levārī
6. levāre
7. levia

SO FAR	BEGINNING WITH THIS LESSON
-two principal parts of verbs	-the other more principal parts
-verb tenses built on first two principal parts	-verb tenses built on third and fourth principal parts of verb

MAINTAIN

-kernel, connector and modification information
-morphology
-expectations
-et cetera

Readings

1. He falls/fell into the pit, which he himself dug.
2. God caused the storm, and they are scattered.
3. Adam, the first man, damned the centuries with the/because of the apple/fruit.
4. Aelius was seized with a disease and got well. But when he saw Doctor Simplicius, he died.

Narrative reading

Hercules, the son of Alcmena and Jupiter, once upon a time lived in ancient Greece. Juno, the queen of heaven, did not like Alcmena, and wanted to kill the infant Hercules. She therefore sent two fierce serpents. In the middle of the night, the serpents came into the bedroom of Alcmena. Hercules was sleeping with his brother in the bedroom. The brother was lying in a cradle, but Hercules was lying in a large shield. Now the serpents approached the shield and moved it. And so Hercules was aroused from sleep.

Directions: Given the following dictionary entries, identify each of the
       items below. Be sure to list part of speech and include all
       possibilities.

I.   dūcō, dūcere, duxī, ductus, -a, -um: to lead
          dux, ducis, m.: a leader

1. dūcī
2. duce
3. dūcere
4. ducibus
5. ductī sunt
6. duxit
7. dūcitur

II.   alō, alere, aluī, altus, -a, -um, alitus, -a, -um: to feed, nourish
          agō, agere, ēgī, āctus, -a, -um: to do, act, drive, lead

1. alunt
2. ēgit
3. alī
4. aluit
5. agit
6. agunt
7. alta est

Narrative reading

The frogs lived in broad waters; they were free, but they were not happy. With a loud shout they sought a king from Jupiter.

Jupiter laughed and threw into the water a little log which frightened the frogs with its loud sound. The log lay for a long time in the water. By chance one of the frogs thrust her head from the water and looked at her king. Then she called out/summoned other frogs. The frogs put aside their fear and with great speed climbed up on the log. They cursed because the log was a useless king. And so they sought another king from Jupiter.

Then Jupiter sent a horrible serpent. The serpent seized the frogs one by one with his fierce tooth. The frogs were affected with great fear and the fear suppressed even their voice. Finally they sent a brave frog to Jupiter. "No longer," she said, "do the frogs want a king. They seek help."

Jupiter, because the frogs did not accept the good king (that is, the log), refused (to give) help, and did not take away the serpent.

And so the frogs, because they did not endure their good fortune, now endured bad fortune.

SO FAR	BEGINNING WITH THIS LESSON
-Clauses have one of three kernel types.	-two new kernel types
-expectations	-new expectations at kernel level within clause
-semantically/syntactically oriented lists of verbs	-new lists of verbs
-case uses of nominative and accusative	-new case uses
-pronouns	-demonstrative pronouns

MAINTAIN

-your list

Required readings

1.   The Celts are called in the Latin language Gauls.
2.   An intemperate sick person makes the doctor cruel.
3.   Anger is brief madness.
4.   Anger makes a stupid man out of a wise man.
5.   Every beginning is difficult.

Optional readings

6.   Old age is a disease.
7.   Virtue is the one and only nobility.
8.   Fortune is blind.
9.   In flight death is disgraceful; in victory it is glorious.
10.   There is nothing new under the sun.
11.   In all things the first beginning is hard.

Directions: Given the following dictionary entries, identify each of the
     items below. Be sure to list part of speech and include all
     possibilities.

I.   timidus, timida, timidum: timid
            timor, timōris, m.: fear, alarm
            timeō, timēre, timuī: to fear

1. timuit
2. timōrem
3. timida
4. timidō
5. timentur
6. timērī
7. timōre

II.   brevis, breve: short
            breviō, breviāre, breviāvī, breviātus, -a, -um: to shorten, abbreviate
            breviārium, breviāriī, n.: a summary, abridgement, abstract

1. brevī
2. breviat
3. brevia
4. breviāria
5. breviāvit
6. breviāta sunt
7. breviāriō

SO FAR	BEGINNING WITH THIS LESSON
-Sentences can have more than one clause. So far, clauses are on an equal level.	-A sentence may have clauses which are not on an equal level, i.e., main and dependent/subordinate.
-several types of adverbial modifiers--syntactic equivalents	-a new type: a dependent clause
-Clauses have kernels and possibly connectors and modifiers.	-Dependent clauses too have kernels and possibly connectors and modifiers.
-part of speech: coordinating conjunction	-new conjunction: subordinating conjunction
-expectations	-Dependent clauses raise expectation of a main clause.

ALL NEW

-clause markers

MAINTAIN

-your list

Required readings

1.   As spring brings flowers, so study brings honors.
2.   Many lose their own things, while they eagerly seek things belonging
      to others.
3.   If a blind man leads a blind man, both fall.
4.   Quintus loves Thais. Which Thais? The one-eyed Thais. Thais doesn't
      have one eye; he doesn't have two eyes.
5.   No one loves his country because it is big, but because it is his own.
6.   While the cat sleeps, the mouse rejoices.

Optional readings

7.   A woman smells right, when she does not smell at all.
8.   Often the powerful man oppresses the just man as the greedy wolf
      oppresses the lamb.
9.   While stupid people avoid faults, they run into the opposite faults.
10.   Your property is in danger, when the wall nearby is on fire.

Narrative reading

Iphicles, the brother of Hercules, cried out in a loud voice; but
Hercules, a brave boy, immediately took the serpents in his little hands, and
pressed hard with great force. The serpents were killed by the boy. His
mother Alcmena, when she heard the scream, aroused the father, Amphitryon,
from sleep. The father, after he lighted a lamp and grabbed his sword,
hastened to the boys. In the bedroom he saw a wonderful sight; for Hercules
was laughing and showing the dead serpents.

Answers to Latin questions

    S11, 1 Dum docent
    S11, 3 Crassus
    R11, 1 ut vēr dat flōrem
    R11, 3 Sī caecus caecum dūcit
    R11, 5 Quia magna est

Supplementary Exercise, Lesson 11

Directions: Given the following dictionary entries, identify each of the
    items below. Be sure to list part of speech and include all
    possibilities.

I.   condiciō, condiciōnis, f.: condition
        condicō, condīcere, condixī, condictus, -a, -um: to agree, to promise

1.   condīcunt
2.   condīcere
3.   condiciōne
4.   condiciōnem
5.   condīci
6.   condīcuntur
7.   condīxērunt

II.   fragilis, fragile: fragile, easily broken
       fragōsus, fragōsa, fragōsum: broken, rough, uneven

1. fragilī
2. fragōsā
3. fragilia
4. fragōsō
5. fragilis
6. fragōsum

SO FAR	BEGINNING WITH THIS LESSON
Adverbial modifiers	-new types of adverbial modifiers
-case uses of accusative	-new case uses of accusative
-prepositions patterning with ablative case	-prepositions patterning with accusative case
-semantic features/categories influencing interpretation of words/phrases	-new semantice features influencing interpretations

MAINTAIN

-your list

Required readings

1.   Among the blind the one-eyed man rules.
2.   After a disaster the memory (of it) is another disaster.
3.   In time of war the laws are silent. (Martial law is declared.)
4.   Publius Scipio was brought back home.
5.   Curius leads four elephants to Rome.

Optional readings

6.   After a loss who is not wise?
7.   Sometimes the stable is repaired after serious loss.
8.   The horse is prepared for war, but victory is given by the Lord.

Narrative reading

Hercules as a young man lived in the city Thebes. King Creon honored Hercules with great honors; he gave his daughter to him in marriage. After a few years Hercules fell into a rage and killed his own children. After a short time he was brought back to sanity, but he was affected with great grief because of that crime. And so he hastened to the Delphic oracle. There the priestess, after she formed a plan, sent Hercules to King Eurystheus. Hercules was held by Eurystheus in servitude for many years. Eurystheus imposed twelve labors upon him. In this way Hercules was able to atone for such a great crime.

_____

Supplementary Exercise, Lesson 12

Directions: Given the following dictionary entries, identify each of the items below. Be sure to list part of speech and include all possibilities.

I.   fundō, fundere, fūdī, fūs.us: to pour
         fundō, fundāre, fundāvī, fundātus: to lay the foundation; to fix, confirm

1. fundī
2. fundārī
3. fundit
4. fundat
5. fūdit
6. fūsum est
7. fundātur

II.   verberō, verberōnis, m.: a scoundrel, rascal
          verbum, verbī, n.: a word

1. verberōnēs
2. verba
3. verberōne
4. verbō
5. verberōnem
6. verbum
7. verberōnibus

SO FAR	BEGINNING WITH THIS LESSON
-Sentences may have clauses which are not on an equal level. Some are dependent adverbial clauses.	-Some dependent clauses are adjectival clauses. -Some dependent clauses are noun clauses.
-Adjectives modify nouns.	-Relative clauses are adjectival modifiers of nouns.
-There are syntactic equivalents of nouns, e.g., substantive adjectives.	-Noun clauses as syntactic equivalent of nouns.
-pronouns	-relative pronouns
-Clause markers are conjunctions.	-Clause markers include relative pronouns.

ALL NEW

-concept of indefiniteness

MAINTAIN

-your list

1.   Romulus founded a city which he called Rome from his own name. He
       chose one hundred old men whom he called senators because of their old
       age.
2.   A plant which is often transplanted does not become strong.
3.   Whoever speaks for an innocent person is eloquent enough.
4.   Caesar builds a wall from Lake Geneva, which flows into the Rhone
       river to the Jura mountain range, which separates the Sequanians from
       the Helvetians.
5.   Stupid people condemn what they don't understand.
6.   Whoever says what he wishes (to say) quite often hears what he doesn't
       wish (to hear).

Optional readings

7.   The gate which leads to perdition is broad and spacious, and there are
       many who enter.
8.   Whoever captures is (himself) captured. (This means if you hunt a
       lion, you may get eaten yourself.)
9.   Whoever becomes wise through another's difficulties, becomes wise in a
       happy fashion. (This means: he doesn't have to pay the price of
       learning through his own trial and error.)
10.   Not all people who have a lyre are lyre players.
11.   Where the person who accuses (is the person who) judges, violence, not
       law, prevails.

Narrative reading

       In a forest near Mycenae there lived a lion which was making the
valley of Nemaea unsafe and dangerous. Hercules immediately made a journey
(went) into the forest which the lion inhabited. He soon found the lion and
bent his bow; the arrows did not pierce its hide which was very thick. Then
Hercules seized a big club and struck the lion. But in vain! Finally he
seized its neck with his own hands and pressed it with great force. After a
short time the beast was deprived of breath (died). Hercules took off the
lion's skin which he afterwards wore for a garment. The dead body he carried
to Eurystheus, who was terrified by such great courage. But all the other
people, when they heard about the death of the lion, were happy.

Supplementary Exercise, Lesson 13

Directions: Given the following dictionary entries, identify each of the
     items below. Be sure to list part of speech and include all
     possibilities.

I.   quī, quae, quod (pron.): who which, what, that
            quiēs, quiētis, f.: rest, repose; quiet peace

1. quā
2. quiēte
3. quiētibus
4. quibus
5. quiētem
6. quae
7. quod

II. nōmen, nōminis, n.: a name
     nōminō, nōmināre, nōmināvī, nōminātus: to nominate; to mention, report

1. nōminatur
2. nōmen
3. nōminārī
4. nōmināvit
5. nōminātī sunt
6. nōminibus
7. nōminō

Narrative reading

Once upon a time many people were sitting in the Circus Maximus
watching a performance in which gladiators fought against beasts. The
gladiators had swords and other weapons. Finally they killed all the animals
and departed from the arena. Soon one man alone, who had no weapons, entered
the arena. A huge lion, which came into the arena from another gate, ran
quickly toward the wretched man, when he suddenly stopped and lay down at the
man's feet. All the spectators asked one another: "Why didn't the lion kill
the man?"

The poor man, Androcles by name, told a strange story in the arena in
the presence of the emperor and the spectators. He had been a slave for many
years. Finally he fled from the villa of his cruel master and came into a
cave. While he was sleeping, a big lion also came into the cave. The lion
approached Androcles and showed its foot which was pouring forth blood.
Androcles saw between its toes a big thorn which he drew out. He took care of
the foot and the lion lived for a long time in the cave with Androcles.

After many days Roman soldiers captured Androcles and dragged him to
his cruel master, who took him to the city and sent him into the arena.
Afterwards soldiers also captured the big lion, which had lived with
Androcles, and led it to the city where it was sent into the arena. But the
lion did not kill Androcles because it loved him.

After all the spectators heard the strange story, they were very happy
and the emperor gave their freedom both to Androcles and to the lion.

Often Androcles, the lion's doctor, walked with the lion, the man's
friend, in the streets where spectators watched them with great delight.

Answers to Latin questions

1.   In Circō Maximō
2.   Spectāculum in quō gladiātōrēs contrā bēstiās pugnābant.
3.   Apud imperātōrem et spectātōrēs
4.   Multōs annōs
5.   Dum Androclēs dormit
6.   In arēnam (in Circum Maximum) in urbem
7.   Quod leō Androclem amāvit
8.   Postquam fābulam mīram audīvērunt

SO FAR	BEGINNING WITH THIS LESSON
-parts of speech	-a new subclass of part of speech: verb OR, if you prefer, a new part of speech
-noun-adjective agreement by case, number, gender	-noun-participle agreement by case, number, gender
-adjectival modifiers	-the participle: a new adjectival modifier
-dependent clause with finite verbs and subject in the nominative	-dependent clauses with non-finite verbs and subject in any case
-Adjective raises expectation of noun-head.	-Participles raise expectations of noun-head.

ALL NEW

relative time

MAINTAIN

-your list

Narrative reading

Hercules, ordered by Eurystheus, hastened with his friend, Iolaus, to the Lernaean lake in which the Hydra lived. The Hydra was a monster, which had nine heads. At first Hercules, bending his bow, shot arrows which did not pierce the monster's hide. Then, seizing its neck with his left hand, he began to cut away its nine heads with his right hand. But in vain! New heads, two in place of a single head, immediately began to grow. Then finally our hero made a new plan. With his friend he cut down trees and, after a fire was made from the pieces of wood, with great effort he burned the necks with burning torches. New heads no longer began to grow from these necks. The Hydra was killed, and Hercules made his arrows poisonous (death-bringing) with the blood of the monster.

Supplementary Exercise, Lesson 14

Directions: Given the following dictionary entries, identify each of the items below. Be sure to list part of speech and include all possibilities.

I.   vox, vōcis, f.: voice, cry, utterance
        vocō, vocāre, vocāvi, vocātus: to call, to invite

1. vōcem
2. vocō
3. vocātō
4. vocāntī
5. vocēs
6. vocātīs
7. vocāntibus

II.   scrībō, scrībere, scrīpsī, scrīptus: to write
        scriptor, scriptōris, m.: author, reporter, narrator

1. scrīptā
2. scriptōre
3. scrīpsērunt
4. scrībēns
5. scriptōribus
6. scrībentibus
7. scriptōrem

SO FAR	BEGINNING WITH THIS LESSON
-partipial clause as part of another clause	-participial clause as a separate clause in the sentence
-adverbial modifiers	-a new adverbial modifier: the ablative absolute
-participial clauses with noun-head and participle in any case	-noun-head in ablative case only
-case uses of nouns in ablative	-new case use: subject of ablative absolute clause

MAINTAIN

-your list

Narrative reading

After the Hydra was killed, Eurystheus, thoroughly frightened (with fear), ordered Hercules to bring back a certain deer. This deer, which had horns of gold and feet of bronze, ran very fast. Hercules, when he saw the deer in the woods, began to run with all his might (his greatest strength), and he didn't leave time for rest (sleep). Finally, after he had run for a whole year, he caught the beast, breathless from running, and carried it back alive to Eurystheus.

When this third labor was finished, Eurystheus ordered other labors in which Hercules captured animals which harmed human beings. In the fourth labor Hercules with greatest difficulty led to the king a boar that had been caught in a trap. In the sixth labor, with the goddess Minerva helping, he destroyed with his poisonous (deadly) arrows the Stymphalian birds which with their savage beaks and sharp claws overpowered human beings and devoured many. After these birds had been killed, Hercules in the seventh labor took back alive from the island of Crete to Greece a bull captured with great difficulty. Whereupon (with this having been done), Hercules undertook the eighth labor. He conquered the horses of Diomedes, which lived on human flesh, and led them to Eurystheus.

The fifth labor was accomplished by mental effort, not by physical strength. Hercules cleaned the stables of Augeas, which had not been washed for thirty years. With two rivers turned through the stables, Hercules easily completed the task in one day.

Supplementary Exercise, Lesson 15

Directions: Given the following dictionary entries, identify each of the items below. Be sure to list part of speech and include all possibilities.

I.   fluō, fluere, fluxī, fluxus: to flow
         fluctus, fluctūs, m.: a flood, wave; turbulence

1. fluente
2. fluctū
3. fluxa est
4. fluctum
5. fluunt
6. fluentibus
7. fluxīs

II.   obsēs, obsidis, m.: hostage
         obsideō, obsidēre, obsēdī, obsessus: to besiege, surround; to occupy

1. obsidentibus
2. obsessā
3. obsidibus
4. obsidente
5. obsidem
6. obsēdit
7. obsidērī

Narrative reading

When the eighth labor had been completed, Eurystheus ordered Hercules to get the belt of Hippolyta, requested by his daughter. Hippolyta, who was queen of the Amazons, warlike women, was willing to hand over the belt; and so Hercules was preparing to set sail. However the other Amazons, aroused by Juno, made an attack upon Hercules' ships. Hercules, forced to fight with these women, easily won and, after the belt had been seized, returned to the city of Mycenae.

After this labor had been accomplished, Hercules was ordered to get the cattle of Geryon. Geryon was a giant with three bodies, who lived in faraway Spain. Because the journey was so long, Hercules, as the story is, with the god Apollo helping, set sail in a golden bowl. With his lion's skin stretched out for a sail, he arrived in a short time in Spain.

After he had climbed a mountain, Hercules caught sight of the cattle, guarded by a shepherd with a large body and by a two-headed dog. This dog, barking fiercely, made an attack upon Hercules, but Hercules who fought with great courage soon killed with his club both the dog and the shepherd. Now he was challenged by Geryon to a fight and, bending his bow, he shot only one arrow through the three bodies of the giant. After Geryon was killed, Hercules first returned the golden bowl to Apollo, then began to lead the cattle through Europe to Greece. Finally, after other adventures, Hercules, exhausted by the long journey, arrived in the city of Mycenae.

Latin questions

1.   Fīlia Eurysthei
2.   Hippolytā zōnam trādere volente
3.   Jūnō
4.   Zōnā captā
5.   Postquam montem ascendit
6.   Lātrāns
7.   Clavā
8.   Gēryone occīsō

English to Latin sentences

a.   Sagitta in auram emissa non redit.
b.   Deus magna curans parva neglegunt.
c.   Deo adjuvante, Hercules iter incepit.
d.   Nono labore confecto, Hercules tres alios labores difficiles suscepit

SO FAR   BEGINNING WITH THIS LESSON

-cases of the noun   -a new case

-uses of nouns in each case   -uses of nouns in dative case
                                             -as kernel parts
                                             -as modifiers

-kernel types   -2 new kernel types with noun in dative

-adverbial modifiers   -new adverbial modifiers: non-kernel
                                          occurrences of the dative

MAINTAIN

-your list

Required readings

1.   Whom(ever) Fortune favors has many friends.
2.   Many things are lacking to poverty, everything is lacking to greed.
3.   God resists the arrogant, however he gives grace to the humble.
4.   No one is a good man except one who is good to all.
5.   The sun shines for all.
6.   No person has everlasting prosperity.

Optional readings

7.   That which is pleasing to many people is guarded with the greatest danger.
8.   A woman who marries many men is not pleasing to many men.
9.   Like pleases like, whether happy, sad, poor, wise, or foolish.
10.   No one is free who is a slave to his body.
11.   For God, for King, for Country.
12.   To each person his own is beautiful.
13.   A word to the wise is enough.
14.   For intemperate people life is short and old age is unusual.
15.   Nothing is sure for mankind.

Narrative reading

When the tenth labor was finished, Eurystheus imposed upon Hercules an eleventh labor. He had to bring back (the) golden apples from the garden of the Hesperides. The Hesperides were beautiful nymphs to whom these apples had been entrusted by Juno. Other men, led on by the desire of gold, had tried without success to carry away the apples. The task was very difficult. For the garden, in which the apples were, was surrounded by a high wall. A dragon, who had a hundred heads, and who never slept, guarded the gate of the garden. Moreover the location of the garden was entirely unknown to Hercules. Although the task was very difficult, nevertheless Hercules decided to obey Eurystheus. He made many journeys through many lands, but was not able to find out anything about the location of the garden. Finally he arrived in a faraway land which was near the Ocean. In that place he found Atlas, a giant of huge body, who was holding up the sky on his shoulders. Hercules sought aid from him. Because Atlas was the father of the Hesperides, he knew the location of the garden and wanted to be a help to Hercules, but he very much feared the dragon. However Hercules, with an arrow shot over the wall, killed the dragon immediately. Then he undertook the task of holding up the sky, while Atlas was away.

Hercules waited several days for the return of Atlas and he did not hear any report about his return. Finally, alarmed by the long delay, he saw him returning with three apples. However Atlas did not give the apples to Hercules, because he himself wanted to hand them over to Eurystheus. This did not please Hercules, who made a new plan: Atlas, as Hercules requested, took back the weight of the sky, while Hercules put a pillow on his shoulders. Then Hercules took the apples and, with great thanks given to Atlas, hastened to go toward Greece.

Hercules did not return to Greece by a direct way. First he went across Libya, where the giant Antaeus forced travellers to fight with him; in this way he killed them. Not only was Antaeus a strong and experienced athlete, but, as often as he touched the earth, his strength was restored to him. Because Hercules did not want Antaeus to harm travellers any longer, he challenged him to a fight. The fight was long and difficult; his mother Earth was a help to Antaeus. Finally Hercules lifted Antaeus up above the ground; he pressed his ribs hard and broke them. In this way he did not spare Antaeus, but brought death to him. After Antaeus had been killed, Hercules proceeded again toward Greece, and after a long time arrived in the city of Mycenae, where he handed over the golden apples to Eurystheus.

Supplementary Exercise, Lesson 16

Directions: Given the following dictionary entries, identify each of the items below. Be sure to list part of speech and include all possibilities.

I.   honor, honōris, m.: honor, distinction
            honōrō, honōrāre, honōrāvi, honōrātus: to honor, respect, decorate

1. honōre
2. honōrī
3. honōrārī
4. honōrantī
5. honōrātō
6. honōrantibus
7. honōrātur

II.   salūs, salūtis, f.: health, safety
            salūtō, salūtāre, salūtāvī, salūtātus: to greet, to pay respects

1. salūtantī
2. salūtātī
3. salūtī
4. salūtāns
5. salūtem
6. salūtantur
7. salūtātīs

SO FAR	BEGINNING WITH THIS LESSON
-cases of the noun	
	-formal introduction of genitive
-genitive as part of dictionary listing	
-uses of nouns in each case	-uses of noun in genitive case
-adjectival modifiers	-noun in genitive as adjectival modifier

Required readings

1. The whole world is the temple of the immortal gods.
2. The discord of the classes is the poison of the city. (In Rome there were ordines: the patricians, the knights, and the common people.)
3. No one of mortals is wise at all hours.
4. Whoever paints the flower does not paint the flower's fragrance.
5. Pleasant is the memory of past troubles.
6. Romulus founded a city which he called Rome from his own name. He chose one hundred old men in accordance with whose advice he did all things and whom he called senators because of their old age.
7. Misfortune is an opportunity for bravery.

Optional readings

8. Rome is the capital of the world.
9. The safety of the people is the supreme law.
10. He whose poems no one reads does not write.
11. In an evil situation a good mind is half of the evil.
12. Fortune is the mistress of human affairs.
13. Necessity is the mother of the arts.
14. One's fatherland is the common parent of everyone.

When the golden apples were brought back to Eurystheus, one labor was left which was the most difficult of the twelve labors. For Eurystheus ordered Hercules to drag Cerberus from Orcus, Pluto's kingdom, from which no one had ever returned. Besides Cerberus there was a monster, which had three heads encircled by fierce serpents. Hercules nevertheless hastened to carry out the commands of king Eurystheus. "No task," he said to himself, "is difficult for Hercules!"

And so he made a journey into Laconia. Here there was a cave which gave an entrance to Orcus. With the help of Mercury and Minerva Hercules descended without delay to Orcus and soon arrived at the bank of the river Styx. Because there was no bridge across this river, the ghosts of the dead were accustomed to being carried across by Charon who waited at the bank with his little skiff. Hercules immediately climbed into the boat, but Charon did not want to untie the boat because of the great weight of Hercules. Finally terrified by the threats of Hercules, Charon took him across the river.

After he crossed the river Styx, Hercules, guided by Mercury and Minerva, came into Pluto's dwelling place. Pluto received him kindly, and gladly gave him the opportunity which he was seeking. "But," Pluto said, "it is necessary to capture and carry away Cerberus without weapons, and afterwards to bring it back into Orcus." Hercules not without great danger seized Cerberus immediately and with the greatest effort dragged it to the city of Eurystheus. This done, Eurystheus, very frightened, ordered Hercules to take the monster back into Orcus without delay.

So, contrary to everyone's expectations, those twelve labors which Eurystheus had ordered were finished within twelve years and Hercules, finally freed from slavery, returned with great joy to the city of Thebes.

_____

Supplementary Exercise, Lesson 17

Directions: Given the following dictionary entries, identify each of the items below. Be sure to list part of speech and include all possibilities.

I. jūstitia, jūstitiae, f.: justice
    jūstitium, jūstitiī, n.: judicial holiday, a suspension of the courts

1. jūstitiā
2. jūstitae
3. jūstitia
4. jūstitiŏ
5. jūstitium
6. jūstitiam

II.   index, indicis, m.: informer, indicator
          indicō, indicāre, indicāvī, indicātus: to point out, disclose, make known

1. indicēs
2. indicat_
3. indicātī
4. indicem
5. indice _
6. indicantī
7. indicārī
8. indicī

Narrative reading

Here, hidden in a deep recess was a cave which, inaccessible to the
rays of the sun, the horrible face of the half-man Cacus occupied. The earth
was always (both) warm from fresh slaughter and the faces (mouths) of men
fastened to the tall doors were hanging pale with dreadful dried blood. This
monster had Vulcan as his father; he, vomiting from his mouth his (Vulcan's)
black fires (smoke) was carrying himself along with his huge mass (body). At
last, time brought even to us hoping for it the help and arrival of a god. For
the great avenger, Hercules, proud because of the slaughter and spoils of
three bodied Geryon, was present and as victor was driving his huge bulls
(oxen) this way, and the cattle were occupying the valley and the river.

SO FAR	BEGINNING WITH THIS LESSON
-verbs in third person	-verbs in first and second person
-subject-verb agreement for person and number	-first and second person agreement
-pronouns	-personal pronouns

Required readings

1. We place a happy life in security of mind. (Our happiness lies in peace of mind.)
2. I think, therefore I exist.
3. We lose what is sure while we seek what is unsure.
4. You should change your spirit, not your environment.
5. Daylight rules me, the shadow (of death) rules you.
6. I am a Roman king and above grammar.

Optional readings

7. Difficult, easy, agreeable, disagreeable you are the same person. Neither can I live with you nor without you.
8. My Rome praises, loves, recites my litte books. All (toga) folds hold me, every hand holds me. Look! A certain person blushes, turn pale, is stunned, is gasping, is hateful. I want this. Now my poems please us (me).
9. Fidentinus, it is my little book that you are reading. But when you read badly, it begins to be yours.
10. I do not like you, Sabidius, and I can't tell you why. Only this can I say. I don't like you.

Directions: Given the following dictionary entries, identify each of the
        items below. Be sure to list part of speech and include all
        possibilities.

I.   quaerō, quaerere, quaesīvī, quaesītus: to look for, search for, ask
            quaestiō, quaestiōnis, f.: examination, inquiry, investigation

1. quaesītīs
2. quaestiōnibus
3. quaestiōnem
4. quaestiōnum
5. quaesīvistī
6. quaerī
7. quaeris

II.   laus, laudis, f.: praise, glory; fame
            laudō, laudāre, laudāvī, laudātus: to praise

1. laudēs
2. laudās
3. laudāvistis
4. laudātis
5. laude
6. laudī
7. laudantibus
8. laudātōs

<u>SO FAR</u>   <u>BEGINNING</u> <u>WITH</u> <u>THIS</u> <u>LESSON</u>

-passive verbs in third person

-all persons of the verb in   -all persons in passive voice
active voice

-pronouns   -reflexive pronouns, intensive pronouns

Required readings

1. All things are changed and we are changed with them. (All things
    change and we change with them.)
2. Not for one's self, but for one's country.
3. Whoever conquers himself in victory, conquers twice.
4. This machine has been built (for use) against our walls.
5. All Gaul is divided into three parts.

Narrative reading

One of the cattle returned the call, and beneath the deep cave
bellowed and, although guarded, disappointed the expectations of Cacus. But
at this point Hercules seizes with his hand his weapons and his wooden club
burdened with knots, and by running makes for the high places of the lofty
mountain.

Then for the first time our people saw Cacus fearing and disturbed in
his eyes; swifter than the southeast wind he flees immediately and makes for
the cave; fear added wings to his feet.

Directions: Given the following dictionary entries, identify each of the
    items below. Be sure to list part of speech and include all
    possibilities.

I.   accūsō, accūsāre, accūsāvī, accūsātus: to reproach, find fault with
            accūsātor, accūsātōris, m.: accuser, prosecutor, plaintiff

1. accūsor
2. accūsātōrum
3. accūsanti
4. accūsātur
5. accūsāminī
6. accūsāvistī
7. accūsātōrem
8. accūsātō
9. accūsātōrī

II.   studium, studiī, n.: study, eagerness
            studeō, studēre, studuī: to be eager, be diligent, to take pains with

1. studia
2. studēs
3. studērī
4. studentēs
5. studiō
6. studētis
7. studiōrum

SO FAR	BEGINNING WITH THIS LESSON
-morphology of passive voice verbs	-verbs with passive morphology but active meaning
-pronouns	-demonstrative pronouns
-adjectives	-special adjectives

Required readings

1. Many people fear rumor (what is said about them), but few fear their conscience.
2. While I talk, the hour flies.
3. Rome has spoken; the case has been finished.
4. We go where our will leads each one (of us).
5. Not because things are difficult do we not dare (to act) but because we do not dare (to act), things are difficult.
6. A son is often accustomed to be similar to his father.

Optional readings

7. Gemellus seeks Maromilla's marriage, desires, pursues, and urges her, and gives (her) presents. Is Maromilla so beautiful? NO, nothing is uglier. What then is sought in her and what is pleasing? She coughs. (Her life expectancy is short.)
8. Labienus likes, admires, and adores himself alone. He not only like himself alone, he also alone likes himself.

Narrative reading

      But the cave and the enormous palace of Cacus appeared exposed and the dark caverns lay open far within. Therefore Hercules from above with his weapons pursues him (Cacus) suddenly caught in the unexpected light and enclosed in the hollow rock (and roaring unaccustomed words), and he calls to his aid all weapons and attacks him with branches and huge stones. He (Cacus) however (for there is no longer left any flight from danger) vomits forth from his throat an enormous cloud-of-smoke, amazing to tell about, and wraps his house in a blinding fog.

Supplementary Exercise, Lesson 20

Directions: Given the following dictionary entries, identify each of the items below. Be sure to list part of speech and include all possibilities.

I.   ūtor, ūtī, ūsus: to use
           ūsus, ūsūs, m.: use, exercise, enjoyment

1. ūsuum
2. ūteris
3. ūtēns
4. ūsus
5. ūsū
6. ūsī estis
7. ūsuī
8. ūtiminī

II.   patior, patī, passus: to suffer, endure; allow
           pateō, patēre, patuī: to stand open, lie open; be open

1. patēns
2. patiēns
3. patimur
4. passī sumus
5. patuī
6. patentī
7. patuimus
8. patēris

Lesson 21

SO FAR	BEGINNING WITH THIS LESSON
-use of infinitive as complementary infinitive (infinitive as part of the verb of a kernel)	-another use of the infinitive--as a verbal noun (infinitive as noun equivalent and therefore in subject or complement function in a kernel)
-semantically/syntactically oriented lists of verbs	-a new list of verbs

Required readings

1. No one can govern except whoever can also be governed.
2. It is pleasant and proper to die for one's country.
3. It is foolish to complain about adversity where the fault is yours.
4. He whom many fear ought to fear many.
5. It is wretched to desire death and not to be able to die.
6. Death demands all things; to die is one's fate, not a punishment (it is a law, not a punishment to die).

Optional readings

7. Both to do and to suffer brave deeds is the Roman way.
8. Those who remove friendship from life seem to remove the sun from the world.
9. Fortune makes foolish whom it wishes to destroy.
10. Not to feel one's misfortunes is not characteristic of a human being (human), and not to endure them is not characteristic of a man (manly).
11. It is the function of art to conceal art. (A true artist makes the performance appear easy.)
12. It is one thing to write a letter, another thing to write history, the one to a friend, the other for all people.

Narrative reading

      Hercules in his intelligence (mind) did not endure this and he threw himself with a headlong leap through the fire where the most smoke is making a wave and the enormous cave seethes with the black cloud (of smoke). Now he (Hercules) seizes Cacus (who is) vomiting useless fires in the darkness and enfolded him into a knot, and clinging to him he squeezes his eyes (which have been) made to protrude and his throat (made) dry with blood. With the doors torn away the dark house is opened up immediately and the cattle that had been dragged away and the robbery that had been denied (covered up) are revealed to the sky, and the shapeless body is dragged out by its feet.

―――――――――――――

Supplementary Exercise, Lesson 21

Directions: Given the following dictionary entries, identify each of the items below. Be sure to list part of speech and include all possibilities.

I.   laborō, laborāre, laborāvī, laborātus: to work
        labor, laboris, m.: toil, hardship

1. laborantibus
2. laboribus
3. laborem
4. labore
5. laborāre
6. laborāvērunt
7. laborum

II.   lītus, lītoris, n.: shore, beach
        līs, lītis, f.: quarrel, argument; lawsuit

1. lītora
2. lītēs
3. lītum
4. lītorum
5. lītibus
6. līte
7. lītorī

SO FAR   BEGINNING WITH THIS LESSON

-parts of speech   -a new part of speech (gerund)--or a
                                            new subclass of an old part of speech
                                            (verb: gerund)

                          _____

-infinitive as verbal noun   -gerund as verbal noun

                  _____

-noun morphology   -limited morphology of gerund

                          _____

Required readings

1.   For a person doing nothing, the day is long.
2.   Human beings learn to act badly by doing nothing.
3.   There is always an opportunity for reading, but not always for
        listening.
4.   The time of life is short; but it is long enough for living right and
        honorably.
5.   My loins hurt from sitting, my eyes from looking, from waiting for the
        doctor.

Optional readings

6.   26 lines from Plautus
7.   An orator is a good man, experienced in speaking.
8.   All things turn out fortunately by being vigilant, by acting and by
        planning well.
9.   One man by delaying restored the state to us.
10   There can be no just reason for anyone for taking arms against his
        country.
11.   As a horse was born for running, an ox for plowing, a dog for hunting,
        so man was born for two things: for understanding and for acting.

Prologue:

In Syracuse, there was a certain merchant, advanced in years. To him two twin sons were born. When the boys were already seven years old, their father loaded a big ship with much merchandise. The father put one twin upon the ship, (and) he carried this twin with him to Tarentum for a buying trip. He left the other twin at home with his mother. The boy wandered away from his father among the crowd. A certain merchant from Epidamnus was there, he took the boy and carried him away to Epidamnus. His father, however, after he lost the boy, lost heart, and because of his sorrow, he died a few days later in Tarentum.

After a messenger returned to Syracuse, (reporting about this event), the grandfather changes the name for this other twin: both twin brothers have the same name. That merchant from Epidamnus, who stole that other twin boy, adopts him as a son for himself and gave him a wife provided with a dowry, and he made him his heir, when he himself died. Now, that twin who lives in Syracuse, will today come to Epidamnus with his slave in order to search for this twin brother of his.

All the citizens believe the stranger to be the citizen Menaechmus and the courtesan, the wife and the father-in law call him Menaechmus. Finally, these brothers recognize each other in turn.

Supplementary Exercise, Lesson 22

Directions: Given the following dictionary entries, identify each of the items below. Be sure to list part of speech and include all possibilities.

I.   condō, condere, condidī, conditus: to found, establish
          respondeō, respondēre, respondī, respōnsus: to answer

1. respondī
2. conditō
3. condendī
4. respondendō
5. respondit
6. respōnsīs
7. condendō

II.   sentiō, sentīre, sēnsī, sēnsus: to feel, experience, perceive
          fundō, fundere, fūdī, fūsus: to pour

1. sentiēns
2. fūsī
3. sentiendō
4. fundentem
5. sentientī
6. fundī
7. sentīris

SO FAR	BEGINNING WITH THIS LESSON
-dependent clauses	-exclusively noun, rather than adjective or adverb
-All dependent clauses (except noun relative clauses) have been modifiers.	-Noun clauses are kernel items.
-All clauses have their own kernels, finite or non-finite.	-Kernels in the new clauses of 1. 23 are non-finite with an infinitive as verb. (Previous non-finite kernels contained participles as verbs.)
-Infinitives have occurred in two syntactic settings.	-two new constructions using infinitives
-Certain verbs raise the expectation of a complementary infinitive.	-Two new lists of verbs raise expectations of either objective infinitive construction or indirect statements.
-There are direct statements. -There are direct commands. (Latin direct commands occur in lesson 28.) -There are direct questions.	-There are indirect statements. -There are indirect commands. -There are indirect questions. (Latin indirect questions occur in 1. 30.)
-Infinitive or infinitive clause is treated as part of a kernel and not a separate entity.	-Kernel of infinitive clause of new embedded utterances is overtly identified (and represented as a separate item on a kernel chart.)
-Infinitive as objective infinite is translated as an infinitive.	-Infinitive in an indirect statment is translated as finite verb, not as an infinitive.

Required readings

1. We often see that the victor is overcome by the conquered one.
2. No learned man (no one learned) ever said that a change of plan was an inconsistency.
3. And indeed I remember that Teucer, banished from his native lands, came to Sidon seeking new kingdoms.
4. Whatever I said I wanted to say to you, I will say.

Optional readings

5. Plautus Selection
6. You, who have the face of one swimming under water, say that beautiful girls are burning with love for you.
7. Alexander said, "Everybody swears that I am the son of Jupiter, but this wound declares that I am a human being."
8. This is your sweetheart whom you told me that you loved?

Plautus: selection to be read after Lesson 23

Pen. For that person doesn't feed persons, but brings them up and revives them. No one provides a better medicine. That man imagines that he is cursing his wife, (but) he is cursing me. For, if he is dining away from home, he is punishing me, not his wife. Men. I. You couldn't have come more at the right time for me than you are coming.

Men. I. Say that I am a very charming guy. Pen. I am saying it: you are a very charming guy. Men. I. I stole this stole from my wife. Nor it will be carried away to my girlfriend. For me, for you and for her I will order dinner to be prepared now. Men. I. Do you know what I want you to take care of? Erot. I know. I will take care of whatever you will want. Men. I. Then order dinner to be prepared at your house for the three of us.

Directions: Given the following dictionary entries, identify each of the
items below. Be sure to list part of speech and include all
possibilities.

I.   puteus, puteī, m.: a well
        putō, putāre, putāvī, putātus: to consider, think

1. putandī
2. putantī
3. puteum
4. putor
5. puteīs
6. putāvērunt
7. putantibus
8. putās

        vīvo, vīvere, vīxī, vīctūrus: to live, be alive
        vīvus, -a, -um: living, alive

1. vīvō
2. vīvendō
3. vīvae
4. vīventēs
5. vīvī
6. vīxistī
7. vīvente
8. vīvis

Lesson 24

SO FAR	BEGINNING WITH THIS LESSON
-finite verbs and participles built on imperfective and perfective stems	-infinitives built on perfective stems
-relative time regarding participles	-relative time regarding infinitives

ALL NEW

-back-shift

Direct and indirect speech

11.73

Indirect speech

The difference between direct speech and indirect (or reported) speech is shown in:

> He said: 'I am very angry' (DIRECT SPEECH)
> He said that he was very angry (INDIRECT SPEECH)

In the case of indirect speech, the words of the speaker are subordinated, in the form of a *that*-clause, within the reporting sentence. In the case of direct speech, his speech is rather 'incorporated' within the reporting sentence by means of quotation marks, and retains its status as a main clause. Nevertheless, notionally, the 'incorporated' speech has the function of an element in the clause structure of the reporting sentence. In the above case, for example, it is the notional direct object of *said*. Cf:

> *What* he said was '*I am very angry*'.

Structurally, the reporting clause, in direct speech, may be classed with comment clauses (11.65–66). It may occur before, within, or after the speech itself. Except when it occurs in initial position, there is likely to be an inversion of the subject and a reporting verb in the simple present or past tense:

> 'I am your friend,' $\begin{cases} \textit{John said} \\ \textit{he said} \\ \textit{said John} \end{cases}$

Inversion is unusual and archaic, however, when the subject of the reporting clause is a pronoun: . . . *said he*. The medial placing of the reporting clause is very frequent:

> 'Of course,' said Mr Jones, 'we're very grateful'

from Grammar of Contemporary English, Quirk, Greenbaum, Leech and Svartvik (Longman Group Ltd: 1972) pp.785-787

The lack of change in case (4) is explained by the observation that if a verb is already in the past perfect form, it already expresses 'past in the past', and no further back-shift to 'past in the past in the past' can be expressed through the grammar of the English verb.

11.75
Exceptions to back-shift

Bearing in mind that back-shift is part of the natural temporal 'distancing' that takes place when we report what was said in the past, we should not be surprised that the rule of back-shift can be ignored in cases where the validity of the statement reported holds for the present time as much as for the time of utterance:

'I *am* a citizen, not of Athens, but of the world,' said Socrates
→ Socrates said that he *was* a citizen, not of Athens, but of the world
'Nothing *can* harm a good man,' said Socrates
→ { (a) Socrates said that nothing *could* harm a good man
    (b) Socrates said that nothing *can* harm a good man

The first statement uttered by Socrates applied only in Socrates' own lifetime, and since from the vantage point of a modern reporter, it deals with what is now past, it has to be reported by application of the back-shift rule. The second statement, on the other hand, is a universal assertion which, if it was true for Socrates' lifetime, should also be true today. We can therefore report it either by (a) applying or (b) ignoring the back-shift rule.

Note
Just as 'distancing' can be avoided, in some circumstances, by not back-shifting the verb, so with pronouns and other forms, the change to the more 'distant' meaning (*eg* to 3rd person pronouns) does not always take place, in that the use of forms appropriate to the reporting situation must take precedence over those appropriate to the reported speech situation. Thus 'I am your friend, Bob' will be reported by Bob, the person addressed, as *He said that he was* my *friend*, rather than as *He said that he was* his *friend*, which would be the expected indirect speech version. So also:

'*You* are very kind,' she said to *me* → She told me that *I* was very kind.

The conversion from direct to indirect speech entails var·ous other changes in the form of the clause, including the shift from 1st person and 2nd person to 3rd person pronouns:

'*I*'ll behave *myself*,' he promised
→ He promised that *he*'d behave *himself*

also (sometimes) the change from *this/these* to *that/those*, and from *here* to *there*:

'*I* live *here*,' he explained → He explained that *he* lived *there*

The most important alteration takes place, however, in the verb phrase: this is the change of tense that is referred to as BACK-SHIFT and is discussed in detail in 11.74 below. These changes collectively represent the DISTANCING effect of indirect speech.

Note
[a] In popular narrative style, the substandard inversion *says I* is sometimes heard.
[b] In journalistic writing, a reporting clause with inversion sometimes occurs even in initial position: *Declared tall, nineteen-year-old Napier: 'The show will go on.'*

11.74
Back-shift
Back-shift takes place when any reported matter is introduced by a reporting verb in the past tense. In these circumstances, the shift from direct to reported speech is accompanied by a back-shift of verb as follows:

DIRECT	BACK-SHIFTED
(1) present	→ past
(2) past	
(3) present perfect	→ past perfect
(4) past perfect	

The explanation of the term 'back-shift' should now become clear: if there is (semantically) a shift into the past in the reporting clause, there is a corresponding shift into the past (or if necessary, further into the past) in the reported clause. Examples of each part of the rule are:

(1) 'I *am* tired,' she complained
   → She complained that she *was* tired
(2) 'The exhibition *finished* last week,' explained Ann
   → Ann explained that the exhibition *had finished* the preceding week
(3) 'I*'ve won* the match already!' exclaimed our friend
   → Our friend exclaimed that he *had won* the match already
(4) 'The whole house *had been ruined*,' said the storyteller
   → The storyteller said that the whole house *had been ruined*

Required readings

1.   I wanted to be able to endure (her death), and I will not deny that I
      have tried. (Orpheus speaks about the death of Eurydice.)
2.   Postumus, you always say that you will live tomorrow, tomorrow (you
      say).
3.   To have begun is half of the deed.
4.   And poets do this in comedies: they say that all things were/have
      been carried on in Athens.
5.   Either he is here or I say that he will be here immediately.

Optional readings

6.   Plautus Selection
7.   A young (man) hopes that he is going to live a long time.
8.   All want to know, but no one wants to pay the price.
9.   There was indeed great terror in Carthage, and they believed that
      Scipio would suddenly attack Carthage itself.
10.   Laocoon there first before everyone with a great crowd accompanying
      (him) in hot haste runs down from the top of the citadel and says from
      a distance, "O wretched citizens, what is this great madness? Do you
      believe that the enemy has sailed away? Or do you think any gifts of
      the Greeks are without treachery?"
11.   I think that what I said today for a joke, that will turn out to be
      serious.
12.   After the end of Augustus was near, few cared for the blessings of
      freedom, some feared war, others desired war. (People said) that
      Agrippa was not equal in age or experience to such a great task; that
      Tiberius Nero was mature in years, but showed many signs of cruelty
      and arrogance. Meanwhile the health of Augustus grew worse, and
      certain ones began to suspect Livia. But in Rome the consuls,
      senators, and knights were rushing into servitude.
13.   This man does not deny that this was done and then he says that he
      will do it.

Plautus: selection to be read after Lesson 24

<u>Mess.</u> This is the 6th year since (after) we have departed from Sicily. The Histrians, the Spaniards, the Massilians, the Illyrians, all the upper sea and foreign Greece and all the Italian shores, where the sea touches, we have visited. We are seeking a dead man among the living. <u>Men. II.</u> I am seeking whoever can tell me that he knows that my twin brother is dead. But otherwise while I am alive I'll never stop following the pursuit. He is most dear to me.

<u>Mess.</u> Why don't we return home? Are you listening, Menaechmus? When I examine the wallet, it is very small. Unless we return home, you will be sorry, as long as you keep seeking your twin. In this city, there live playboys and very many drunkards, also blackmailers and callgirls. To this city the name Epidamnus was given, because nobody comes here without damage. <u>Men. II.</u> I will guard against this. Just give me the wallet. <u>Mess.</u> What do you mean? <u>Men. II.</u> I am worried about your words. <u>Mess.</u> What are you worrying about? <u>Men. II.</u> I am worrying about damage in Epidamnus. You are a great lover of women, Messenio, I, however, am an easily angered man. If I will hold it, neither will you do wrong, nor will I be angry with you. <u>Mess.</u> Haven't I told you that there are here very many sharpers? <u>Men. II.</u> Order yourself to be exorcised for my money, for I surely know that you are insane. <u>Cook.</u> I'll go inside and tell Erotium that you are standing here nearby. <u>Mess.</u> For I believe that a callgirl is living over there, as at least that insane fellow said who just went away from here. <u>Men. II.</u> By Hercules, you are warning me properly. If you have properly guarded against her then indeed will I know that I have warned you properly.

Supplementary Exercise, Lesson 24

Directions: Given the following dictionary entries, identify each of the
    items below. Be sure to list part of speech and include all
    possibilities.

I.   capsa, capsae, f.:_a box (esp. for books), bookcase, satchel
            capiō, capere, cēpī, captus: to take, seize

1. cēpistis
2. cēpisse
3. capī
4. capsam
5. capsā
6. capientis
7. captō
8. captōs esse
9. capsīs

II.   dūcō, dūcere, dūxī, ductus: to lead
            dux, ducis, m.: leader

1. ducī
2. dūcī
3. dūcendī
4. dūcentēs
5. ductō
6. dūxisse
7. ductūrum
8. ducis
9. dūcis

SO FAR	BEGINNING WITH THIS LESSON
-adjectives and adverbs in positive degree	-adjectives and adverbs in comparative and superlative degrees
-case uses of ablative	-new case use--ablative of comparason (one of few uses of personal nouns in ablative)
-case uses of genitive	-new head/signal for partitive interpretation
-vocabulary knowledge of individual items from correlative sets	-pairs of items as correlatives

Required readings

1. Whoever scorns the smaller gifts loses the bigger ones.
2. Nothing is greater in human affairs than philosophy.
3. There are as many people as there are opinions.
4. Nothing is more pleasant than the light of truth.
5. The good opinion of men is safer than money.
6. The more people have, the more they want.
7. Who is friendlier than brother to brother?

Optional readings

8. The law does not care about trifles (least important things).
9. The eyes are more trustworthy than the ears.
10. Hunger is the best cook.
11. Outer (overt) acts indicate inner secrets.
12. Certain remedies are more dangerous than the perils (they may prevent).
13. The higher the ascent is, the harder the descent.
14. I have never felt that I was as loved as (I am) now.
15. Where concord exists, there victory exists.
16. As the master is, such is the slave.
17. A person dies as often as he loses his loved ones.

Supplementary Exercise, Lesson 25

Directions: Given the following dictionary entries, identify each of the items below. Be sure to list part of speech and include all possibilities.

I.   nōbilis, nōbile: well-known, famous, renowned
         nōbilitās, nōbilitātis, f.: celebrity, fame; high birth, nobility

1. nōbilitātem
2. nōbiliōribus
3. nōbilī
4. nōbiliōre
5. nōbilium
6. nōbilēs
7. nōbilia

II.   dīvitiae, dīvitiārum, f. pl.: riches, wealth
         dīves (dīvitis): rich

1. dīvitis
2. dīvitiās
3. dīvitēs
4. dīvitiārīs
5. dīvitiae
6. dīvitium
7. dīvitissimī

SO FAR

-knowledge of imperfective stem

-present imperfective tense

BEGINNING WITH THIS LESSON

-two new tenses on same stem

Required readings

1. This was, is, and will be: like seeks like for himself.
2. And now the voices of men and dogs were silent, and the moon on high began to drive her steeds of night.
3. Now I in one jump will cleverly capture two wild boars.
4. To few people was fidelity dearer than money.
5. I am what you will be.
6. A woman either loves or hates; there is no third.

Optional readings

7. Plautus Selection
8. In your light we will see the light.
9. Now the Roman victor held the whole world.
10. True reason will have more force with me than the opinion of the crowd.
11. Whoever has spared evil people harms good people.
12. We hate whomever we have harmed.
13. As long as the Coliseum stands (will stand) Rome will stand too; when the Coliseum falls (will fall) Rome will fall too; when Rome falls (will fall) the world will fall too.
14. Perhaps at some time it will be a pleasure to remember even these things.

Plautus: selection to be read after Lesson 26

Erot. Where is he, who the cook says is standing in front of the house? And I see him. Now I'll go up to him and speak to him of my own accord. "My darling, it seems astonishing to me that you stand here outside. Since this house is more yours than your own house. Everything has been prepared as you have ordered and wished . . . The dinner has been prepared here, as you have ordered. Men. II. With whom is this woman speaking? Erot. Surely with you. Men. II. What business have you ever had with me or what business have you with me now? Erot. Why then did you order me to prepare dinner for you? Men. II. I ordered you to prepare dinner? Erot. Certainly, for you and your parasite. Men. II. For what parasite? Certainly, this woman is not quite

sane. _Erot._ For Peniculus. _Men. II._ Who is that Peniculus? _Erot._ He, who came with you, when you brought me the stole, which you did steal from your wife. _Men. II._ What is going on? I have given you a stole, which I have stolen from my wife? Are you sane? _Penic._ I have lived more than 30 years... Never have I seen a worse and more criminal act that today when I got myself mixed up with the assembly. But what do I see? Menaechmus with a garland is stepping outside! The dinner has been removed, I'll watch the man, then I'll step up and address him. _Men. II._ By the immortal gods, to what man have you ever on one day given more good, a man who didn't dream of it. I have eaten, I have drunk, I have kissed. I have brought away this stole! She says that I have given her this stole and that I have stolen it from my wife.

Supplementary Exercise, Lesson 26

Directions: Given the following dictionary entries, identify each of the
      items below. Be sure to list part of speech and include all
      possibilities.

I.   custōdiō, custōdīre, custōdīvī, custōdītus: to guard
          custōs, custōdis, m. and f.: a guard, keeper, attendant

1. custōdiēbāris
2. custōdiendō
3. custōdientibus
4. custōdibus
5. custōdient
6. custōdītae estis
7. custōdīvērunt
8. custōdīverās

II.   lībertās, lībertātis, f.: freedom, permission, absence of restraint
          līberō, līberāre, līberāvī, līberātus: to free, set free

1. līberābiminī
2. līberātī erunt
3. līberātae erant
4. līberābātis
5. lībertātis
6. lībertāte
7. lībertantī
8. lībertandī

151

SO FAR   BEGINNING WITH THIS LESSON

-knowledge of past, present, future
times
-knowledge of imperfective vs.   -two new tenses on perfective stems
imperfective aspects
-knowledge of perfective stems
-present perfect tense

Emphasize same person endings as before.

Required readings

1. Whoever despises (will have despised) glory, will have true glory.
2. You will quickly break the bow if you always hold (will have held) it
    tense, but if you relax (will have relaxed) it, it will be useful when
    you want it.
3. What had been faults are customs.
4. As long as you are (will be) successful, you will count many friends; if
    times are (will have been) cloudy; you will be alone.
5. In whatever judgment you judge (will have judged), you will be judged.

Optional readings

6. I have lived and I have completed the course which Fortune had given,
    and now the great image of me will go beneath the earth.
7. While we are talking, envious time will have passed by.
8. A wolf and a lamb had come to the same river, driven by thirst. The
    wolf stood above, and the lamb stood far below him (on the bank of the
    river). Then the robber (the wolf), aroused by wicked hunger (jaws,
    throat) introduced an excuse for a quarrel. "Why", he said, "have you
    made the water muddy for me (while) drinking it?" The woolly lamb
    fearfully (fearing), said in reply (contra): "How can I, I ask, be
    doing what you are complaining about, Wolf? The water is flowing down
    from you to my drinking place (drinkings)." The wolf, defeated by the
    force of the truth, said: "Six months ago you spoke to me
    maliciously." The lamb answered, "I had not even been born." "By
    Hercules," he (the wolf) said, "it was your father who said evil
    things to me." And so, with unjust slaughter he tears to pieces the
    lamb that he had seized.

    This story was written because of those men who oppress the innocent
    with false charges.

Supplementary Exercise, Lesson 27

Directions: Given the following dictionary entries, identify each of the
items below. Be sure to list part of speech and include all
possibilities.

I.   reddō, reddere, reddidī, redditus: to give back
        reditus, reditūs, m.: a going back, return

1. reddidisse
2. reditū
3. reddēmur
4. reditūs
5. reddideritis
6. reddiderat
7. reddidērunt
8. reddiderint

II.   inveniō, invenīre, invēnī, inventus: to find, com upon
        inventum, inventī, n.: an acquisition

1. inventa
2. inventō
3. inventum erat
4. invenientur
5. inveniendō
6. invenientī
7. inventa eram
8. inventus erō

Lesson 28

SO FAR	BEGINNING WITH THIS LESSON
-direct statements	-direct commands
-direct questions	

-indicative mood   -imperative mood (subjunctive mood in next lesson)

-five cases of the noun   -a new case of the noun

Required readings

1. You who have read our names, farewell.
2. I have found the harbor. Hope and Fortune, farewell. You have made sport with me enough; now make sport with others.
3. Learn to bear good fortune well.
4. Listen, look, be silent, if you wish to live in peace.
5. If you want peace, prepare for war.
6. Save me, I will save you.

Optional readings

7. Plautus Selection
8. I have a lawsuit (my lawsuit is) not about assault nor murder nor poisoning, but it is about three little goats. I am complaining that these are missing because of the theft of my neighbor. The judge demands that this be proved to him. In a loud voice and with (gestures of) your whole arm you sound off about Cannae and the Mithradatic war and the false oaths of the Carthaginian madness and Sulla and Marius and Mucius. Now speak, Postumus, about my three little goats.
9. Catiline, go on where you have begun (to go). Now at last go out of the city. The gates are open, go.

Men. II. Since I realized that she is making a mistake, I began to agree with whatever she had said. I kept saying the same. I never have had such a good time for less cost. Penic. I'll step up to the man. What are you saying, you fellow flightier than a feather, you rascal, you? Men. II. Young man, I ask you, what business have you with me? By Pollux, I have never before this day either seen or known you. Penic. Menaechmus, wake up? Don't you know me. Don't you know your own parasite? Didn't you steal today from your wife that stole there and didn't you give it to Erotium? Men. II. By Hercules, I don't have a wife, and I didn't give a stole to Erotium and I didn't steal a stole. Penic. Now I'll tell your wife the whole story. All those insults will fall back on you. You won't have eaten your dinner unpaid for.

Supplementary Exercise, Lesson 28

Directions: Given the following dictionary entries, identify each of the items below. Be sure to list part of speech and include all possibilities.

I.   mittō, mittere, mīsī, missus: to send, let go
         mītis, mīte: soft, gentle; mature, ripe

1. mitte
2. mītī
3. mītissimae
4. mittiminī
5. mīserat
6. mītius
7. mītēs

II.   dūcō, dūcere, dūxī, ductus: to lead, guide
         dux, ducis, m.: leader

1. ducem
2. dūcar
3. dūxeritis
4. dūxistis
5. ducēs
6. dūcēbātis
7. dūcere

SO FAR	BEGINNING WITH THIS LESSON

-finite verb forms in
  indicative mood
  imperative mood
	-finite verb forms in
	  subjunctive mood

-independent verb expressing "fact"	-independent verb suggesting an act/state as "possible," "willed" or "wished for"

Required readings

1. If you do anything, do it prudently, and regard the outcome.
2. Let (the person) who has given a favor keep quiet; let (the one) who has received it tell.
3. Therefore should I, carried away by the winds, leave my sister and brother, my father and the gods, and my native soil? (Spoken by Medea, wrestling with her overpowering love for Jason, who is the enemy of her family.)
4. While we live, let's (really) live.
5. Let us say what we feel; let us feel what we say: our speech should agree with our lives.
6. No woman is more unhappy than I (am) nor could any woman seem more unhappy.
7. Judges, what am I to do? Where am I to turn (myself)?

8.   Plautus Selection
9.   Plautus Selection No. 2
10.   You should endure and not blame what can't be changed.
11.   Let justice be done, even thought the heavens collapse (let the heavens fall).
12.   Let us eat, live, and be merry; there is no pleasure after death.
13.   Love conquers all things; and we should yield to love.
14.   The people want to be deceived; let them be deceived.
15.   I wish that your actions would correspond to the words that you are saying.
16.   Who could not know the noble descent of the Trojans, the city of Troy, its deeds of valor and its heroes or the fires of such a great war?
17.   Let others wage wars; you, happy Austria, marry! For the kingdoms Mars gives to others, Venus gives to you.
18.   Whoever loves may he prevail; may he perish who doesn't know (how) to love; may he perish twice as much whoever forbids (to) love.
19.   Gaudeamus Igitur

        Let us rejoice,
        while we are young:
        after an agreeable youth,
        after an annoying old age,
            the earth will have us.

        Where are those who
        were on earth before us?
        Go to the upper world
        Go to the lower world
            Where they have already been.

        Our life is short,
        in a short time it will be finished;
        Death comes quickly,
        it seizes us fiercely;
            noone will be spared.

        Let the university live;
        Let the professors live;
        Let any part you please (live);
        Let any parts you please live:
            Let them always flourish (be in flower).

        Let the state live
        and the person who rules it.
        Let our city live
        Let this fraternity live
            that has gathered us here.

        Let our Alma Mater flourish,
        that has educated us,
        and gathered together
        our dear comrades who
        have been planted here and there
            in scattered regions.

Men. I. May all the gods send him to perdition! The way he has ruined this day for me today! And me too, who (because I) looked with my eyes into the forum at any time today. I have ruined a wonderful day. I ordered dinner to be prepared. My girlfriend is expecting me, I know. As soon as it was possible, I hurried to go away to this place from the forum. She is now angry with me, I am sure. The stole will pacify here, the stole which I gave her, which I today stole from my wife and which I delivered to this Erotium.
Penic. What are you saying? Matr. That I am badly married to a bad man.
Penic. Do you hear well enough what that man says? Matr. Well enough.
Men. I. If I were smart, I would go inside from here, where I have a good time. Penic. Wait: it will rather be worse. Matr. Did you think that you could do those disgraceful things secretly? Men. I. What is this all about, wife? Matr. Are you asking me? Men. I. Do you want me to ask him? Matr. Take your hands off me! Penic. Go on, you! Men. I. Why are you cross with me! Matr. You ought to know. Penic. He knows, but the bad man pretends (that it isn't so). Men. I. What is this about? Matr. The stole. Men. I. The stole? Matr. The stole, a certain person . . . Penic. What are you scared of? Men. I. I am scared of nothing. Penic. Except of one thing: the stole strikes you pale. Go back there. Men. I. Where shall I go back to? Penic. To the embroiderer indeed, I think. Go, bring the stole back.
Men. I. Which stole is this? Matr. Truly, by Castor, I am a wretched woman.
Men. I. Why are you a wretched woman. Explain it to me. One of the slaves hasn't done wrong, has he? The maids or the slaves aren't talking back to you, are they? Speak out, it won't go unpunished. Matr. You are talking nonsense. Men. I. You are certainly angry at one of the servants? Matr. You are talking nonsense. Men. I At least you are not angry with me? Matr. Now you are not talking nonsense.

Selection 2, to be read after Lesson 29

Men. I. The wife thinks that she has treated me badly when she shut me out outside, just as if I didn't have another better place to which I would be admitted. If I don't please you, I must bear it, but I will please this Erotium, who will not shut me out from her, but shut me in at home with her. Open up and someone call Erotium out in front of the door. Erot. Who is looking for me here? Men. I. Somebody more an enemy to himself than to your youth. Erot. My Menaechmus, why are you standing in front of the house. Follow (me) inside. Men. I. Wait! Do you know whay I am coming to you? Erot. Certainly, you come to make love. Men. I. No, by Pollux, that stole which I gave to you a little while ago, give it back to me: the wife has found out the whole story, as it has happened. Erot. Indeed I gave you that (stole) a little while ago. Men. I. You gave me the stole? You never did. For indeed I, after I gave it to you a little while ago and went to the forum, I am coming back now (only) and I see you now (only). Erot. I see your plan. You want to cheat me, because I entrusted the stole to you. Men. I. I don't want to cheat you. I am telling you that my wife has found out the whole story. Erot. You brought it to me of your own free will, you gave it to me as a gift. Now the same thing, you ask it back. I'll put up with it. Have it for yourself, take it away, use it, either you or your wife, cram it down into your money-boxes. You will not set foot inside after this day unless you bring money, you cannot lead me on for free. Men. I. Hey you, I'll tell you, wait! Come back! She has gone away, she has shut the house. Now I am most shut out. Neither at my home nor at my girlfriend's house no credit is given to me.

Supplementary Exercise, Lesson 29

Directions: Given the following dictionary entries, identify each of the
    items below. Be sure to list part of speech and include all
    possibilities.

I.   spērō, spērāre, spērāvī, spērātus: to expect, to hope for
            spēs, speī, f.: hope

1. speī
2. spērantis
3. spērem
4. spem
5. spērābar
6. spērēmur
7. spēs
8. spērāverint

II.   rapiō, rapere, rapuī, raptus: to seize, snatch
             rapax (rapācis): greedy, rapacious; violent

1. rapax
2. rapiās
3. rapiāris
4. rapāciōra
5. rapiendī
6. rapient
7. rapācissimīs
8. rapiunt

SO FAR	BEGINNING WITH THIS LESSON
-verb of <u>independent</u> clause in the subjunctive mood	-verb of <u>dependent</u> clause in subjunctive mood

---

-direct statements and indirect statements	
	-indirect questions
-direct questions	
-direct commands and indirect commands (obj. infinitive)	-(indirect command w/finite clause in l. 31)

-finite noun clauses with verb in indicative mood	-finite noun-clause with verb in subjunctive mood

---

-present imperfective tense of subjunctive	-3 more tenses

-relative time regarding non-finite verbs in embedded clauses	-relative time regarding finite verbs in embedded clauses

Required readings

1.   I want to know what you are doing, what you are waiting for.
2.   Everyone asks whether he is rich; no one asks whether he is good.
3.   "He is a slave." But perhaps he is free in spirit. "He is a slave."
       Will this harm him? Show (me) who is not (a slave). One serves (is a
       slave) to desire, another to greed, another to ambition, all to fear.
4.   You will know who I am from him whom I have sent to you.
5.   A disaster reveals whether you have a friend or (only) a name.

Optional readings

5.   Plautus Selection
6.   Don't ask a fortune teller what God intends. What he decides about
       you, he plans without you.
7.   Then you will learn all your descendants and what city walls will be
       given to you.
8.   A poor man perishes when he tries to imitate a rich man.

       Once upon a time a frog saw a cow in a meadow, and, touched with envy
       of such great size inflated her wrinkled skin. Then she asked her
       children whether she was bigger than the cow. They said no. She (the
       frog) again stretched out her skin with a greater effort, and asked in
       a similar way who was bigger. They said the cow (was). Finally
       angered, while she was trying harder to inflate herself, she lay
       (there) with her body burst. (She burst her body and lay there.)

9.   For neither does anyone except traders go there without purpose nor is
       anything known to them (to these very people) except the seashore and
       those regions which are opposite Gaul. Therefore, with traders
       summoned to him from all sides, he was able to find out neither how
       large the size of the island was, nor what tribes inhabited the
       island, nor what experience in war they had, nor what institutions they
       followed nor what harbors were suitable for a rather large number of
       ships.

Plautus, Selection to be read after Lesson 30

<u>Men. I.</u> For as often as I want to go outside, you are holding me back, calling me back, questioning me, where I am going, what I am doing, what business I have, who I am looking for, what I am carrying, what I have done outside. I have brought a (married) janitor home: thus I must spell everything out, whatever I have done or am doing.

<u>Men. II.</u> But I wonder how that man knows my name. <u>Mess.</u> It's not at all strange, by Hercules. (all girls have this custom: they send little boy slaves and little girl slaves to the harbor. If any foreign ship comes into the harbor, they ask where it is from, what name it has.) <u>Men. II.</u> By Hercules, you certainly warn me properly. <u>Mess.</u> I'll know then that I have you properly, if you will have been on guard properly. <u>Men. II.</u> Just be quiet now for a moment, for the door has creaked. Let's see, who is stepping out from here.

<u>Men. II.</u> This woman indeed, by Pollux, calls me properly by my own name. I wonder a lot, what business this is. <u>Mess.</u> This wallet which you have has given off a whiff to her. <u>Men. II.</u> Any by Pollux, you have warned me properly. Take it now: I will soon know, whether she loves me or my wallet more. <u>Erot.</u> Let's go inside.

Supplementary Exercise, Lesson 30

Directions: Given the following dictionary entries, identify each of the items below. Be sure to list part of speech and include all possibilities.

I.   rogātum, rogātī, n.: a question, interrogatory
          rogō, rogāre, rogāvī, rogātus: to ask

1. rogā
2. rogāta
3. rogāverint
4. rogāvissētis
5. rogāvisse
6. rogātō
7. rogātī sītis
8. rogārent

II.   postulō, postulāre, postulāvī, postulātus: to demand, require
           postulātiō, postulātiōnis, f.: a demand, request, desire

1. postulārētis
2. postulātiōnem
3. postulātus esset
4. postulāverīs
5. postulātiōne
6. postulātī estis
7. postulētur
8. postulābāris

SO FAR	BEGINNING WITH THIS LESSON
-direct and indirect statements -direct and indirect questions -direct and indirect commands	-an indirect command expressed by a finite noun clause
-indirect command expressed by non-finite clause (the objective infinitive construction)	-indirect command expressed by a finite noun clause
-a list of clause markers	-a new clause marker <u>ne</u> and a new meaning of <u>ut</u>
-lists of verbs grouped semantically	-a new list of verbs

Required readings

1. The senate at one time voted that the consul should see to it that the state received no harm.
2. I ask and implore you to help him.
3. You demand, Tucca, that I give you my little books. I will not do it. For you want to sell them, not read them.

Optional readings

4. Plautus Selection
5. You will dine well, my Fabullus, at my house in a few days, if the gods favor you, if you will have brought with you a good and big dinner, not without a beautiful girl and wine and salt, and all (your) laughs. If you will have brought these things, my fine fellow, you will dine well: for your Catullus' wallet is full of cobwebs. But on the other hand you will receive unadulterated love or something sweeter or more elegant: for I will give you an ointment that Venuses and Cupids have given to my girl, and when you smell this, you will ask the gods to make you, Fabullus, all nose.

6. I remember and will always remember what things you have given to me. You say, Postumus, "Why am I silent?" As many times as I begin to tell someone about these gifts, he immediately exclaims: "He himself had told me." Two persons do not do certain things properly: One person is enough for this task (duty). If you want me to talk, you remain silent yourself. Believe me, Postumus, gifts, although enormous, perish because of the talkativeness of the giver.

7. You ask, Quintus, that I give you my poems. I don't have (a copy) but the bookseller Tryphon does. "Will I, a sane person, give money for trifles and buy your poems. I will not act so foolishly" you say. Nor will I.

8. The hours indeed pass and the days and the months and the years, nor does past time ever return nor can it be known what will follow. Whatever time is given to each person for living, he ought to be satisfied with that. For a brief life time is long enough for living right and honorably.

Plautus: selection to be read after Lesson 31

Matr. I'll go to see how soon my husband is coming home. But I see him! I am saved, he is bringing back the stole! Men. II. I wonder, where Messenio is now walking. Matr. Aren't you ashamed to come into my sight with that outfit? Men. II. What is it, what bothers you, woman?
Father. How many times have I explained to you that you should humor your husband, that you shouldn't watch what he is doing, where he is going, what business he has. Matr. He robs me, he secretly carries my jewels to his girlfriend. Father. He does wrong if he does that. If he doesn't do it, you do wrong. Tell me this, Menaechmus, what you are discussing. Men. II. Whoever you are, whatever your name is, old man, I give mighty Jove and the gods as witnesses that I neither have mistreated this woman nor do I know her. If I ever have set foot inside her house where she lives, I pray that I should become of all miserable men the most miserable.

Men. II. Now those people have gone out of my sight, who force me to act
insanely though I am well. Why do I hesitate to depart for the ship? You
all, I ask you, if the old man returns that you won't reveal me, by which
street I have escaped form here.

Supplementary Exercise, Lesson 31

Directions: Given the following dictionary entries, identify each of the
    items below. Be sure to list part of speech and include all
    possibilities.

I.   sinō, sinere, sīvī, situs: to allow
            situs, sitūs, m.: location, station

1. situī
2. sitī
3. sinite
4. sīverātis
5. sinat
6. sitibus
7. sīvissēs
8. sīverit

II.   statuō, statuere, statuī, statūtus: to decide, determine; set up
            status, stata, statum: set, fixed, regular

1. statuētis
2. statiōra
3. statuerāmus
4. statuēbar
5. statius
6. statuissem
7. statuendī
8. statōrum

SO FAR	BEGINNING WITH THIS LESSON
-finite noun clauses with verbs in subjunctive	-two new finite noun clauses: noun result clause and clause of fearing
-semantically/syntactically oriented list of verbs	-new lists

Required readings

1. In the same night it happened that the moon was full.
2. It happened that all the statues of Hermes were destroyed in one night.
3. Caesar brought it about that he held the king under his authority.
4. I am afraid that all my evil deeds have been discovered.
5. I am afraid that she is not deaf.

Optional readings

6. Plautus Selection
7. Plautus Selection No. 2
8. Because of these things it was brought about that the soldiers dared to hold off an attack of the cavalry and were not greatly frightened by their large number.
9. I am afraid that that thing is (will be) great trouble for me.
10. I am afraid that the disease is growing worse.
11. I am awfully afraid that I am changing my name here and am becoming Quintus from (instead of) Sosia. He says he has put four men to sleep: I am afraid that I will increase that number.

Plautus: selection to be read after Lesson 32

Father. My limbs ache from sitting, my eyes from looking, from waiting for the doctor. Doctor. What sickness, did you say, he has? Tell me, old man! Father. But I am bringing you for this purpose, that you tell me and make him well. By Hercules, I beseech you, doctor, do whatever you are going to do. Don't you see the man is mad. Doctor. See that he is brought to my office. There I'll be able to take care of the man. So, call men who can bring him to me. Father. How many are enough? Doctor. Four, no less. Father. They'll be here right away. Doctor. I'll go home. Let them bring him to me. Men. I. What do you want? What are you looking for? Why are you surrounding me? Where are you forcing me to? Where are you carrying me? I am done for. Help, citizens! Mess. I'll never allow you to perish, it is better that I perish. You rascals, you rapists, you robbers. The Four We are done for. Mess. Come on, get away, run off from here to the gallows!

Supplementary Exercise, Lesson 32

Directions: Given the following dictionary entries, identify each of the items below. Be sure to list part of speech and include all possibilities.

I.   dubitō, dubitāre, dubitāvī, dubitātus: to doubt, wonder, hesitate
        dubius, dubia, dubium: doubtful

1. dubitābāminī
2. dubitantibus
3. dubitātī erunt
4. dubitet
5. dubitentur
6. dubitābātis
7. dubiōrēs
8. dubiīs

II.   inferō, inferre, intulī, illātus: to bring in, bring upon
        laevus, laeva, laevum: on the left side; unfavorable, unlucky

1. laevius
2. intulisse
3. intulissem
4. infert
5. laeviōribus
6. inferāmus
7. infereent
8. laeviōrum

<u>SO</u> <u>FAR</u>	<u>BEGINNING</u> <u>WITH</u> <u>THIS</u> <u>LESSON</u>
-adverbial modifiers: finite adverbial clauses	-additional adverbial clauses
-adverbial clauses with verb in indicative	-adverbial clauses with verb in subjunctive
-important lists	-another list: words signalling adverbial result clauses
-relative clauses with verb in indicative	-relative clauses with verb in subjunctive
-relative clauses expressing fact	-relative clauses expressing purpose or characteristic

Required readings

1.	Don't entrust all your belongings to one ship.
2.	We are slaves of the laws so that we can be free.
3.	You should eat and drink in order to live a good life; you should not live only to eat and drink.
4.	He was accustomed to say that no book was so bad that it was not useful in some part.
5.	A general never trusts peace to the extent that he doesn't prepare himself for war.
6.	Indeed the nature of human beings is such (this) that nothing is more pleasing than what has been lost.
7.	What man is there who would say that I said that?
8.	There is nothing said now which has not been said before.
9.	I am the kind of person who has never done anything for my own sake rather than for the sake of my fellow citizens.
10.	You are not the kind of man who wouldn't know what you are.

Optional readings

11.	Plautus Selection
12.	Mirrors were invented so that man might know himself.
13.	You are always pleading law suits, Attalus, and you are always engaging in business (whether) there is (or) isn't anything for you to do, you are always busy. If business affairs and lawsuits are lacking, Attalus, you drive mules. Attalus, so that there won't be anything lacking for you to do, you should drive out your breath of life (die).
14.	Why don't I send you my little books (poems), Pontilianus? So that you won't send me yours, Pontilianus.
15.	Theodorus, do you wonder why I don't give my little books to you, demanding and asking for them so many times. There is a good reason: so that you won't give your little books to me.
16.	One should pray that there be a sound mind in a sound body. Ask for a brave mind without (lacking) the fear of death, which places the end of life among the gifts of nature, which can bear any labor whatsoever, which does not know how to be angry, which desires nothing, and which believes the tasks and cruel labors of Hercules more important than love affairs and banquets and the downy couch of Sardanapallus. I point out what you can give to yourself. Surely the only path of a happy life lies open through virtuous living.

Plautus:	selection to be read after Lesson 33

Men. I.	The others say that I am not who I am and shut me out, out of doors, and this one (= Messenio) kept saying that he is (was) my slave whom I have set free. He says that he will bring me a wallet with money. If he brings it, I will tell him that he can go away from me free, wherever he wishes, in order that he won't ask me for the money, when he has become sane. My father-in law and the doctor kept saying that I was insane. What is going on is strange. Now I'll go to this callgirl, although she is enraged at me, (to see) if I can urge her to give back the stole which I can carry home.

Supplementary Exercise, Lesson 33

Directions: Given the following dictionary entries, identify each of the
    items below. Be sure to list part of speech and include all
    possibilities.

I.   probitās, probitātis, f.: honesty
            probō, probāre, probāvī, probātus: to test, try, examine

1. probantis
2. probitāte
3. probāvistī
4. probā
5. probāvissent
6. probandō
7. probitātī

II.   dīlectus, dīlectūs, m.: a selection, choice, distinction
            dīligō, dīligere, dīlēxī, dīlēctus: to esteem, value, honor

1. dīlectum
2. dīligī
3. dīligēs
4. dilectuum
5. dīlēctō
6. dīligeris
7. dīlectuī

SO FAR	BEGINNING WITH THIS LESSON
-finite adverbial clauses	-more adverbial clauses
-semantic categories of clauses	-three additional semantic categories
-clause markers	-new clause markers and new meanings for old clause markers
-sentences with simple condition (si)	-sentences containing other types of conditions

Required readings

1. If you had kept quiet, you would have remained a philosopher.
2. The country fellow waits until the stream runs by.
3. In order that time could intervene until the soldiers could assemble, he replied to the envoys that he would take time for deliberating.
4. If Democritus were on earth, he would laugh.
5. Provided that he is rich, even a barbarian (foreigner) is pleasing.
6. When Caesar had noticed these things, with a council summoned, he accused them vehemently.

Optional readings

7. Plautus selection
8. Plautus selection

Plautus: Selection 1 to be read after Lesson 34

Men. II. There is no greater joy for sailors, Messenio, to my mind that when they see land far away from the sea. Mess. There is a greater joy, I'll say without cheating, if you arrive and see the land which has been yours.
Mess. If you were looking for a needle, you would have found the needle already long ago, if it was there. We are looking for a dead person among the living, for we would have found him long ago, if he was alive.

Plautus: selection 2 to be read after Lesson 34

Men. I. My true twin brother, greetings. I am your twin. Men. I. Oh greetings, you unhoped for, whom I see many years later. Men. II. Brother, you too, whom I have sought up to this point with many worried (and) efforts and over whom I rejoice that he has been found. Mess. This was it, why this callgirl kept calling you by your name. She was thinking that you were he, I believe, when she called you to dinner. Men. I. For, by Pollux, I ordered dinner to be prepared for me here today behind the back of my wife, from whom I stole the stole out of the house a little while ago. I gave it to her. How did it get to you? Men. II. The callgirl seduced me in here to dinner, she kept saying I had given it to her ... Let's both return home. Men. I. Brother, I'll do as you wish. I'll make an auction here and sell whatever there is. Men. II. So be it. Mess. Do you know what I am asking you? That you give me the job of auctioneer. Men. I. It will be given. Mess. There will be an auction of Menaechmus, definitely in the morning on the seventh day. For sale there'll be the slaves, the furniture, the land, the building, everything, even the wife too will be for sale, if any buyer will come. Now, audience, goodbye and applaud us loudly.

THE END

Supplementary Exercise, Lesson 34

Directions: Given the following dictionary entries, identify each of the
   items below. Be sure to list part of speech and include all
   possibilities.

I.   ordō, ordinis, m.: order, rank, class
          ordinō, ordināre, ordināvī, ordinātus: to arrange, regulate

1. ordinēs
2. ordināverit
3. ordinābātis
4. ordinem
5. ordinārer
6. ordinis
7. ordinātus sīs

II.   ācer, ācris, ācre: sharp
          acervō, acervāre, acervāvī, acervātus: to heap or pile up, amass

1. acervantur
2. ācrius
3. ācrī
4. acervārentur
5. ācerrimīs
6. acerventur
7. ācriōrum

SO FAR	BEGINNING WITH THIS LESSON
-participles	-another participle: the future passive
-metaphrase of gerunds	-same metaphrase for gerundives
-morphology of periphrastic verbs, e.g., _auditus est_	-another periphrastic: the future passive [But _all_ _new_ is the translation which includes the notion of obligation.]
-passive verbs with subjects	-passive verbs without subjects

Required readings

1.   Nothing should be done without reason.
2.   Besides I think that Carthage should be destroyed.
3.   One should deliberate often, decide once.

Optional readings

4.   A wife's fault should either be removed or endured.
5.   There is a time when nothing should be said, a time when something
        should be said, no time however, in which everything should be said.
6.   Reason shows what should be done or what should be avoided.
7.   Least of all should anyone have confidence in very great fortune.
8.   Live, happy people, for whom your fortune has already been achieved;
        we are called from one destiny to another. For you rest has been won;
        no expanse of the sea has to be ploughed through nor do the fields or
        Ausonia, always retreating backward, have to be sought.
9.   Caesar had to do everything at one time: the flag had to be set
        forth, which was the signal when it was necessary to run to arms; the
        signal had to be given with the trumpet; the soldiers had to be
        recalled from the trenchwork; those who had gone a little farther for
        getting material for the rampart had to be sent for; the battle line
        had to be drawn up; the soldiers had to be encouraged; the signal (for
        battle) had to be given.
10.   We are all led on by the desire of praise, and all the best are (each
        best person is) especially influenced by glory. Those very
        philosophers even in those books which they write about condemning
        glory, inscribe their own names; in that very act in which they look
        down upon publication and renown, they want to be given publicity
        about themselves and to be mentioned.

Supplementary Exercise, Lesson 35

Directions: Given the following dictionary entries, identify each of the
    items below. Be sure to list part of speech and include all
    possibilities.

I.   pugnō, pugnāre, pugnāvī, pugnātus: to fight
            pugna, pugnae, f.: a fight, battle, combat

1. pugnā
2. pugnārī
3. pugnēs
4. pugnandī
5. pugnīs
6. pugnantibus
7. pugnātur

II.   voluptās, voluptātis, f.: pleasure
            voluptābilis, voluptābile: pleasant, agreeable

1. voluptātī
2. voluptābilia
3. voluptās
4. voluptābilī
5. voluptābilior
6. voluptātibus
7. voluptātēs